THE AUTISTIC SPECTRUM

By the same author:

Autistic Children: a Guide for Parents (1971)
Early Childhood Autism (editor, 1976)
Aspects of Autism: Biological Research (editor, 1988)
Hospital Closure and the Resettlement of Residents (1989)

THE
AUTISTIC SPECTRUM

A guide for parents and professionals

LORNA WING

Constable · London

For Susan

First published in Great Britain 1996
by Constable and Company Limited
3 The Lanchesters, 162 Fulham Palace Road
London W6 9ER
Copyright © Lorna Wing 1996
Reprinted 1996
ISBN 0 09 475160 9
Set in Linotron Sabon 10½pt by
Rowland Phototypesetting Limited
Bury St Edmunds, Suffolk
Printed in Great Britain by
St Edmundsbury Press Limited
Bury St Edmunds, Suffolk

A CIP catalogue record for this book
is available from the British Library

Contents

PREFACE   11

Part 1 Description of autistic spectrum disorders   15

1   HISTORY   17
    Evolution of ideas on autistic spectrum disorders   21

2   THE NATURE OF AUTISTIC SPECTRUM DISORDERS   24

3   MAKING A DIAGNOSIS   27
    Sub-groups of autistic spectrum disorders   29

4   THE BEHAVIOUR OF CHILDREN WITH AUTISTIC
    SPECTRUM DISORDERS   32
    Behaviour in babies   32
    Behaviour diagnostic of autistic spectrum disorders   34
    Impairments of social interaction   35
        i   *The aloof group*   35
        ii   *The passive group*   36
        iii *The 'active but odd' group*   37
        iv   *The over-formal, stilted group*   37
    Impairments of communication   38
        i   *Using speech*   38
        ii   *Understanding speech*   40

iii   *Intonation and voice control*   42
iv   *Using and understanding non-verbal
      communication*   42
Impairments of imagination   ,   44
Repetitive stereotyped activities   45
  i   *Simple repetitive activities*   45
  ii   *Elaborate repetitive routines*   46
Other features of behaviour   48
Movements   48
  i   *Stereotyped movements*   48
  ii   *Abnormalities of gait and posture*   49
  iii   *Imitating movements*   50
Responses to sensory stimulation   50
  i   *Responses to sounds*   50
  ii   *Responses to visual stimuli*   51
  iii   *Responses to proximal sensations*   52
  iv   *Appetite and thirst*   53
Anxiety and special fears   53
Attention and motivation   54
Special skills   55
Inappropriate behaviour   56
Epileptic fits   58
Changes with growing up   58

5   HOW MANY CHILDREN HAVE AUTISTIC SPECTRUM
    DISORDERS?   60
    Prevalence   60
    Are the numbers increasing?   61
    Age of onset   62
    Numbers of boys compared with girls   63
    Parents' occupations   64

6   CONDITIONS ASSOCIATED WITH AUTISTIC SPECTRUM
    DISORDERS OR AUTISTIC-LIKE BEHAVIOUR   65
    Generalized learning difficulties   66
    Rett's syndrome   68
    Fragile X syndrome   68
    Landau-Kleffner syndrome   69
    Other neurological conditions   69

Contents

Severe hearing impairments 70
Severe visual impairments 71
Developmental language disorders 71
Semantic-pragmatic disorder 72
Disorders of attention, motor coordination and
perception 73
Elective mutism 73
Psychiatric conditions 74
Effects of deprivation 76

7 WHAT CAUSES AUSTISTIC SPECTRUM DISORDERS? 78
Original causes 79
The pathology in the brain 80
Psychological dysfunctions 81

Part 2 Ways of helping 85

8 MAKING SENSE OF TIME AND SPACE 87

9 THE TRIAD OF IMPAIRMENTS 92
Social interaction 92
Developing social contact 92
Expeditions, holidays and social occasions 95
Communication 97
Imagination 98
Resistance to change and repetitive activities 99

10 REDUCING INAPPROPRIATE BEHAVIOUR 103
General principles 104
Temper tantrums and aggression 108
The use of medication 110
Destructiveness and interference with others' possessions 112
Self-injury 113
Restlessness and hyperactivity 115
Socially embarrassing behaviour 116
Special fears 119
Lack of fear of real dangers 122
Stereotyped movements 122

Problems with eating 123
Problems with sleeping 126
Quiet, withdrawn children 127

11 TEACHING BASIC SKILLS 128
General principles 128
The pattern of skill development 130
Encouraging cooperation 130
Toilet training 134
Self-care 135
Helping in the home 137
Toys and games 139
Physical activities 140
Children with profound learning disabilities 141
Physical health 143

12 BABIES WITH AUTISTIC SPECTRUM DISORDERS 146

13 ADOLESCENTS AND ADULTS WHO REMAIN
DEPENDENT 149
Adolescents 149
Inappropriate behaviour 149
Education 150
Leisure activities 151
Sexual development 151
Adults 153
Occupation 153
Leaving home 153

14 THE MORE ABLE CHILDREN, ADOLESCENTS AND
ADULTS 155
Definition and diagnosis 155
Childhood 156
Problems at home and at school 156
Making life easier 157
i *At home* 158
ii *At school* 159
Adolescence 162
Desire for independence 162
Awareness of disability 164

Contents

Friendships and sexual relationships 166
Pressure of exams 167
Adult life 168
Living accommodation 168
Employment 169
Marriage 171
Psychiatric illness 172
Delinquent and criminal behaviour 175
The borderlines with normality 177

15 SISTERS AND BROTHERS 178

16 PROBLEMS FACED BY PARENTS 181

17 THE ROLES OF PROFESSIONAL WORKERS 187
Family doctors 188
Treatment of physical illnesses and disabilities 188
Paediatricians and psychiatrists 189
Diagnosis and medical investigations 189
Discussion with parents 190
Treatment for psychiatric disorders 191
Prescribing medication 192
Dentists 192
Clinical psychologists 193
Assessment 193
Behaviour management 193
Counselling 194
Social workers 194
Educational psychologists 194
Teachers 195
Speech and language therapists 195
Other therapists 196
Counsellors 197
Staff in day centres 198
Residential care staff 199
Advocates of 'curative treatments' 199

18 SERVICES FOR CHILDREN AND ADULTS 201
Diagnosis and assessment 201
Medical services for physical illnesses 202

Psychiatric services 202
Dental services 203
Clinical psychology 204
Social services 204
Practical advice for parents 205
Pre-school units 206
Educational services 207
  Mainstream or special school? 207
  Types of special schools 210
  Residential schooling 212
  Unorthodox educational approaches 213
  Assessment of educational needs and 'statementing' 213
  The National Curriculum 215
Speech and language therapy 216
Physiotherapy and occupational therapy 216
Music and other special therapies 216
Occupational services 216
Respite care 218
Residential care for adults 218
How to find and evaluate services 219
The role of voluntary societies 220
  The National Autistic Society 221
  Local Autistic Societies 223
  Other voluntary bodies 224

POSTSCRIPT 225

READING LIST 226

INDEX 235

Preface

I wrote the first version of this book in 1970. It was then called *Autistic Children: a Guide for Parents*. The present book follows a similar plan to the original but has been almost entirely rewritten. Twenty five years ago, interest was focused mainly on the typical autistic syndrome as described by Leo Kanner. The theory that autism was due to a cold, mechanical style of parenting was still strongly held by many professionals. Little was known about outcome in adult life. Since then, it has been recognized that there is a spectrum of disorders that is much wider than Kanner's syndrome. The fact that the autistic spectrum comprises disorders of development due to physical dysfunctions of the brain is now generally accepted and a great deal is known about outcome in adult life.

There is just as much heated debate as there was in 1970 but the scientific searchlight is currently centred on the specification of diagnostic criteria, the differentiation of sub-groups that might have different causes or methods of treatment, defining the boundaries of the spectrum and investigations into the neuropathology and how this is expressed in psychological mechanisms and overt behaviour. Beyond the range of rational argument controversies rage about a variety of so-called treatments or cures, each of which bursts upon the scene like a rocket and then quietly fizzles out.

The increase in secure knowledge about autistic disorders has not led to any curative methods of treatment. The real advances have been in understanding how to create an environment and a daily programme that minimize the disabilities and maximize the potential skills. This is a solid gain but does not change the underlying neurological and psychological impairments. Research and clinical experience have demonstrated the wide range of outcomes in adult life, from total dependence to independence in spite of residual disabilities. For parents of the most severely affected children it is hard to be presented with the facts about the future. The writer of a book for parents of children and adults of all ages and all levels of ability is faced with a dilemma: how much of the whole picture should be given? But, even if it were desirable, it is becoming increasingly difficult, because of articles, books, videos, TV programmes and feature films, to hide the truth. Most parents *do* want all the facts, negative as well as positive, so that they can form a realistic plan of action.

As in 1970, I have referred throughout to 'parents' in the plural. Unlike 1970, I am now conscious of the growing number of single parents who have children with autistic disorders. References to parents in the plural should be read to mean one parent alone or together with a partner with whom they share the tasks. In addition to all the other changes, the dreaded Political Correctness has cast a long shadow and I have conformed. In the first edition, the term 'autistic children' was used, doctors, psychologists and autistic children were referred to as 'he', and teachers were always 'she'. Now, these automatic assumptions seem wrong, even to one not in the forefront of the PC movement. The current terms are 'children/adults with autism/autistic spectrum disorders'. The pronouns 'they, them and their' are used regardless of singular or plural in order to avoid ascribing gender whenever possible. In the terminology used by the Department for Education and Employment and local education authorities, 'mental handicap' has been replaced by 'learning difficulties', although, to make confusion worse confounded, the Department of Health refers to 'learning disabilities'. In this book, I have chosen to use the DFEE term except when referring to disabilities in general. This new terminology is meant to do away with discrimination. It makes for clumsiness of style and I am not sure what difference it has made in real life to women or to people with disabilities.

Another difference from 1970 is that many books on autistic disorders are now available, some of which are in the reading list at the end. Most deal with particular aspects of the subject. The present book is a general introduction, intended to lead on to more specialized texts. It fills a particular niche because my dual role as parent of a grown-up daughter with autism and a professional with research and clinical experience provides an insight that cannot be obtained from any one of these viewpoints alone. Perhaps this book will enable parents and professionals to understand each other a little better and thereby increase the help that each can give to children and adults with autistic spectrum disorders.

Children and adults with autistic disorders have the same basic patterns of behaviour wherever they live. When parents from different countries meet, cultural barriers melt away and common experiences are shared. The original version of this book is translated into different languages (the latest being Chinese) and has been read by parents and professionals all over the world. I hope that this new book will transcend barriers in the same way as the first.

Part 1

DESCRIPTION OF
AUTISTIC SPECTRUM DISORDERS

·1·

History

It seems likely that there were children and adults with autistic disorders in all their manifestations long before these conditions were recognized and named. Perhaps they were the reason for the ancient legends of 'fairy changeling' children, in which the fairies were believed to steal away a human baby and leave a fairy child in its place. In some versions of the story the changeling was remarkably beautiful but strange and remote from human kind.

Uta Frith, in her book *Autism: Explaining the Enigma*, gives some fascinating examples from legend and history of individuals who were likely to have had various forms of autistic disorders. My favourite is Brother Juniper, from a collection of legends concerning the early followers of St Francis. One example of many stories of this endearing character recounts an incident while he was on a pilgrimage. The citizens of Rome came to welcome him but he ignored them. His attention was taken by a see-saw and he continued to use this long after the amazed crowd had returned home. The stories about him illustrate his complete inability to understand social situations and the feelings of affection mixed with exasperation that he produced in the other brothers.

In January 1801, a French doctor, Jean-Marc-Gaspard Itard, was given charge of a boy about 12 years old, known as Victor the 'Wild Boy of Aveyron', who had been found living wild in the woods and had been finally captured a year before. The child's behaviour was very strange and he was mute. Itard thought that this was because he had been isolated from humans from an early age. Philippe Pinel, another eminent physician of the time, disagreed with Itard. He believed that the boy had had severe generalized learning difficulties from birth. Harlan Lane, a psychologist specializing in the study of speech, hearing and language, collected together Itard's papers on Victor and published them in his book, *The Wild Boy of Aveyron*. Reading the account now, it is possible to see that Victor behaved like a child with autism. All the stories of his behaviour would be familiar to any parent of a child with typical autism living today, despite the time difference of nearly two centuries. Dipping into Itard's account one can find example upon example of which the following are just a few. Victor never learnt to speak. Itard described how, when he wanted a ride in a wheelbarrow, he would pull someone by the arm, put the wheelbarrow handles in their hands, then climb in and wait to be pushed. Itard spent hours trying to teach Victor to play with all kinds of toys and succeeded only in making the boy so impatient with these activities that he destroyed the toys if left alone with them. It was noted that Victor had a 'decided taste for order' and was unhappy until he could return an object that had been moved to its proper place.

Some people have suggested that his behaviour was due to his being isolated from human beings from infancy but, from the available documents, it appears that Victor was first seen in 1797, when he would have been nine or 10 years old. He was naked and lived on nuts, fruit and any root vegetables he could find plus occasional food given to him by local farmers. He had a thick scar across his throat suggesting that someone had tried to kill him. It seems much more likely that he was separated from, or abandoned by, his parents in the troubled times following the French Revolution because he was autistic and difficult to manage.

Itard's story is most interesting and moving and contains details of the way in which he set about teaching the boy. His ideas were passed on to his pupil, Edouard Séguin, and thence to Maria Montessori and still influence methods of special education.

Some years later, in 1809, John Haslam, in England, gave an account of a boy who had had measles severely at the age of one. His subsequent behaviour closely resembled that of the type of child with an autistic disorder who has much repetitive speech and impulsive, aggressive behaviour. He was admitted to Bethlem Royal Hospital at five years of age.

Over a century later, in 1919, an American psychologist, Lightner Witmer, wrote an article about Don, a boy of two years and seven months, who behaved like a child with autism in its typical form and who was accepted at Witmer's special school. Individual teaching over a long period helped this child to make progress in school work and in acquiring practical skills.

These authors described individuals but did not consider whether there were others with similar problems. A step forward in thinking occurred during the first half of the 20th century, when various people wrote about groups of children with strange patterns of behaviour. Each thought he or she had identified a specific condition but there was a great deal of overlap in the features of behaviour they described. In particular, all the children concerned were very abnormal in the way they interacted with other people. The writings of most of these authors are rarely quoted now, apart from those of Leo Kanner and Hans Asperger.

Leo Kanner, in the USA, recognized that a number of children referred to his clinic had in common an unusual pattern of behaviour, which he named 'early infantile autism'. He published his original paper on this condition in 1943. He gave detailed descriptions of the children's behaviour but selected certain features as crucial for diagnosis. These were, profound lack of affective (emotional) contact with other people; intense insistence on sameness in their self-chosen, often bizarre and elaborate repetitive routines; muteness or marked abnormality of speech; fascination with and dexterity in manipulating objects; high levels of visuo-spatial skills or rote memory in contrast to learning difficulties in other areas; an attractive, alert, intelligent appearance. Later, he suggested that the first two of these features were sufficient for diagnosis. He also emphasized that the condition was present from birth or within the first 30 months of life. Kanner believed his syndrome was unique and separate from other childhood conditions." Interest in Kanner's work grew slowly at first and then more rapidly and is now the focus of much research in many different countries.

In 1944, Hans Asperger, in Austria, published his first paper on a group of children and adolescents with another pattern of behaviour now referred to as Asperger's syndrome. The features he selected as important were naive, inappropriate, social approaches to others; intense circumscribed interest in particular subjects such as railway timetables; good grammar and vocabulary but monotonous speech used for monologues, not two-way conversation; poor motor co-ordination; level of ability in the borderline, average or superior range but often with specific learning difficulties in one or two subjects; a marked lack of common sense. He noted that the parents did not observe any abnormality until after three years or until the children started school. Asperger believed that his syndrome was different from Kanner's autism, though he admitted there were many similarities. Asperger published in the German language towards the end of the Second World War and there was a long delay before papers on the subject appeared in the English literature. It is only in the last 10 to 15 years that his work has become well known outside continental Europe.

In 1962, the first voluntary association to be formed anywhere in the world for parents and professional workers concerned with autism was set up in the UK and is now called the National Autistic Society. Although originally the focus was on Kanner's autism, it soon became clear that there were many children who did not precisely fit Kanner's descriptions but who had similar problems and needed similar kinds of help. As a result of the efforts of such societies, with the help of publicity through the media, the existence of autistic conditions has become much better known to the general public, and people with autistic disorders have appeared in fictional stories such as the film *Rain Man*.

There have always been disagreements concerning the defi-

nition of autism and how it relates to other disabling conditions
of childhood, including all kinds of learning difficulties and language impairments. In the 1970s, my colleague Judith Gould and
I decided to investigate these questions. We examined all children
aged under 15 in one area of London (the former borough of
Camberwell) who had any kind of physical or learning disability
or abnormality of behaviour, however mild or severe. We could
identify a group with typical Kanner's autism but found more
who had many features of autistic behaviour but who did not
precisely fit Kanner's criteria. There were a few who had the
pattern described by Asperger, which, at the time we did the
study, was not familiar to us. We now know that, if we had
included children in mainstream schools, we would certainly
have found more with Asperger's syndrome. The main findings
from this study were, first, that Kanner's and Asperger's syndromes are sub-groups among a wide range of disorders affecting
social interaction and communication; second, that these could
be associated with any level of intelligence; third, that they were
sometimes associated with various physical conditions or other
developmental disabilities. It was also clear that learning difficulties could occur without associated autistic disorder even
though they often occurred together.

Evolution of ideas on autistic spectrum disorders

Over the course of time, there have been major changes in ideas
on the nature of autistic conditions. Before there was any understanding of the relationship of brain and behaviour, supernatural
causes were suggested – 'a changeling child' or 'demonic possession'. In the case of Victor, the 'Wild Boy of Aveyron', some
believed he had been abandoned as a baby and, as in the legend
of Romulus and Remus, had been reared by wolves. This explanation has been used for some other recorded cases of children
found living in a wild state, although consideration of the practical details of feeding and rearing a human baby makes it seem
highly unlikely.

Towards the end of the 19th century, the possibility of

'psychosis' occurring in children was suggested by the psychiatrist Henry Maudsley. This word has no precise meaning but tends to be used as a general label for behaviour that is bizarre and strange. Disorders that are now considered to be in the autistic spectrum fitted this description so were classified as 'childhood psychoses'.

In the first decades of the 20th century the theories of the psychoanalysts affected the attitudes of professionals and the public at large. After Kanner published his first paper on 'early infantile autism' many believed that autism was an emotional, not a physical disorder and that the way the parents had brought up their child had caused all the problems. The effect was disastrous – it exacerbated the parents' distress at having a child with behaviour they could not understand, made them feel guilty and damaged any confidence they may have had in their ability to help their child.

It was not until the 1960s that fresh ideas on the nature of autistic disorders began to emerge. Research into normal child development and language disorders, as well as work on Kanner's autism, especially that by Michael Rutter and his colleagues, produced major changes. This work showed that the behaviour of children with autism made sense if viewed as due to disorders of aspects of development starting from birth or the early years of childhood. Growing knowledge of the way the brain functions and the things that can go wrong has made it clear that the causes are physical and nothing to do with the parents' child-rearing methods. Few people now blame parents, but traces of the old ideas still linger among some professionals and some lay people, still causing much unhappiness for the parents who meet these attitudes.

Some child psychiatrists considered that autistic disorders were forms of childhood schizophrenia. However, a series of studies by Israel Kolvin and his colleagues in the 1970s demonstrated the differences between autism and the very rare condition of schizophrenia occurring in childhood.

In the 1970s and 80s, the idea that Kanner's autism was part of a wider spectrum of autistic disorders began to be seriously considered, encouraged, among other studies, by the work in

Camberwell mentioned above and that of Christopher Gillberg and his colleagues in Sweden. The implications for research and clinical practice of this view are still being investigated.

The changes in ideas about autistic disorders can be seen in the history of the two international systems of classification of psychiatric and behavioural disorders. These are the *International Statistical Classification of Diseases and Related Health Problems* (ICD) published by the World Health Organization and the *Diagnostic and Statistical Manual* (DSM) of the American Psychiatric Association. The first editions of the ICD did not include autism at all. The eighth (1967) edition mentioned only infantile autism as a form of schizophrenia and the ninth (1977) edition included it under the heading of 'childhood psychosis'.

The 10th edition of the ICD (1992) and the third (1980), third revised (1987) and fourth (1994) editions of the DSM take the modern view that there is a spectrum of autistic conditions and that they are disorders of development, not 'psychoses'. The name used in both classification systems is 'pervasive developmental disorders'. Most parents in the UK do not like this term and find it confusing. They prefer 'autistic spectrum disorders' and this term will be used in this book.

The nature of autistic spectrum disorders

Once it was recognized that autistic behaviour was a result of problems of development, interest focused on which skills were not developing properly. In order for a baby to become a fully functioning and independent adult, many different abilities have to appear at the appropriate stages and then grow in complexity. At first, many of us working in this field believed that autistic behaviour was due to disorders of language development. This appeared plausible because so many of the children had delayed and deviant language or none at all. It seemed that, if understanding and use of spoken speech and communication by gestures were all affected, this would account for autistic behaviour. At that time, it was hoped that overcoming these specific language problems by some alternative method of communication would produce major improvement. This theory had to be rejected when it was found that some children and adults with autistic spectrum disorders developed good grammar and vocabularies and even used some gestures but still had autistic behaviour.

A clue to the nature of autism came from accounts of the behaviour of babies as remembered by their parents. In infants who are later diagnosed as having autistic disorders, lack of interest in social interaction is often present from very early on, well before the time when speech develops. Studies of normal early development show that there is an inbuilt interest in the sight and sound of other human beings especially, at first, the mother or other carer. There is also a drive to communicate in every possible way, through bodily movements and baby noises, before speech begins, and to respond to communications from others. These inbuilt 'instincts' can be seen from very early in the first year.

In the second year, another aspect of the social skills should begin to emerge – that is, imagination. The child starts to play with toys first for simple sensations, then to use them for their obvious purposes and then for pretend games. The child becomes able to pretend that one object represents another – a box is a bed for a baby doll, or a row of chairs is a bus. Later, children play together and develop complex imaginative games. Imagination enables all kinds of skills to be practised. In particular, it enables a child to pretend to be other people and take on their roles in social play. Playing games of this kind depends upon the child having developed the knowledge, inbuilt but taking time to emerge, that other people have thoughts and feelings – the so-called 'Theory of Mind'. When this has emerged, pretend games help to improve skill in understanding other people that is so necessary for integration into social life.

These abilities are just as dependent upon brain function as all other developmental skills. They are absent or severely impaired in children with autism. In the study in Camberwell, described in Chapter 1, we found that all the children with 'autistic features', whether they fitted Kanner's or Asperger's descriptions or had bits and pieces of both, had in common absence or impairments of social interaction, communication and development of imagination. They also all had a narrow, rigid, repetitive pattern of activities and interests. The three impairments (referred to as the 'triad') and the repetitive activities were shown in a wide variety of ways, but the underlying similarities were recognizable.

There can be no doubt that a yet more fundamental impairment of psychological function underlies the triad. It is likely that there is an inability to put together all kinds of information derived from past memories and present events, to make sense of experiences, to predict what is likely to happen in the future and to make plans. People with autistic disorders do not make sense of the world and find it hard to learn from experience. They find it difficult to organize themselves in time and in space. Uta Frith wrote that they lacked what she called a 'drive for central coherence'. The more complex the incoming information, the harder it is for an individual with an autistic disorder to understand. Human beings are extremely complicated and variable in their speech, movements and reactions, so it is not surprising that impairment of social interaction is a major feature of autistic disorders.

It is possible that, at an even deeper level, there is a disturbance of the normal inbuilt system for assigning different degrees of emotional significance to different experiences. There are various theories concerning how the brain originally assigns emotional value to the biological necessities for survival and reproduction and then, building on these, develops over the years a complex system of values related to the culture in which the individual lives. Whatever the neural mechanisms, it appears that people with autistic disorders are impaired in their ability to distinguish between the important and the trivial. In some of the young children there is indifference even to food. In all those affected, the lack of interest in others is a defining feature. Coupled with this is the idiosyncratic fascination for specific objects or experiences that appear trivial and meaningless to others.

One day we may have tests that demonstrate the nature of the basic problems. For the present, recognizing autistic spectrum disorders has to depend on detecting the triad of impairments because the three impairments can be identified from knowledge of an individual's development and behaviour.

·3·

Making a diagnosis

Despite the fact that the existence of autistic disorders has become much more widely known, there are still difficulties surrounding diagnosis. Most of the children look physically normal. Minor congenital abnormalities, which are reported to be common in the children, do not adversely affect their appearance, which is often very attractive, not least because of the quality of mysterious remoteness. There are no tests yet developed that can be used to make the diagnosis of autism nor any that can tell the difference between sub-groups within autistic disorders. Blood tests, X-rays, brain scans, electroencephalograms (that is, records of the electrical waves from the brain) and other physical examinations cannot give a positive answer to the question, 'Does this child have an autistic disorder?'. Psychological examinations, including the recently developed 'Theory of Mind' tests (see Chapter 7), though helpful in other ways, cannot be used to confirm or refute the presence of an autistic spectrum disorder. There is reason to hope that useful tests will be found but we do not have them at the present time.

In this situation, diagnosis is made by recognizing patterns of behaviour present from early in life. All systems for diagnosis that have been suggested, including the ICD and DSM, agree that the impairments of social interaction, communication and imagination and the rigid, repetitive pattern of activities are crucial diagnostic features. Despite this fundamental accord, disagreements over diagnosis of individual children and adults arise for many reasons, including the following.

1 The impairments can be shown in many different ways, some of which are subtle and not easy to recognize.

2 Autistic spectrum disorders can occur together with any level of general intelligence, from profound disability to well above average.

3 They can occur together with any other physical disability or developmental disorder. Epileptic fits are particularly common.

4 Changes in the behaviour pattern can occur with increasing age.

5 Behaviour can vary according to the environment. It is often worse at home, where parents have many competing demands for their attention, than it is in a well-organized school or clinic.

6 Behaviour can vary depending on the person the child or adult is with. It is always better with an adult who is experienced in working with autistic disorders than it is with inexperienced people or in unstructured groups. Some adults who are high-functioning, including those with the pattern described by Asperger, may show no signs of their impairments in one-to-one situations, including interviews with a psychiatrist. The problems are revealed in their life history, especially in the way they cope with events they find stressful.

7 Education affects the behaviour pattern.

8 Each individual's own personality shines through and influences their behaviour.

Diagnosis depends on compiling a personal history that links together all the available information. Ideally, the history from infancy and a description of the present behaviour should be collected systematically by interview with the parents. A schedule of questions designed to diagnose autistic spectrum disorders should be used so that all important details are covered. In addition, the behaviour of the individual should be observed and a range of psychological tests given. All this takes time to complete – at least two to three hours for the interview alone. If the procedure is rushed and the right questions are not asked, the diagnosis can be missed.

Sub-groups of autistic spectrum disorders

When an autistic disorder is diagnosed, there is the further problem of deciding which sub-group in the spectrum the individual belongs to. Now that the term Asperger's syndrome is being used more widely, parents, and professional workers as well, want to know how it differs from other forms of autism. Since Asperger's group, unlike Kanner's, includes mainly those with average or high levels of ability, the main question is how to tell Asperger's syndrome from high-functioning Kanner's autism. There is no simple answer. It is possible to find some individuals who have all the features described by Kanner and others who fit Asperger's syndrome perfectly (see Chapter 1). However, there are many who fit neither of these syndromes precisely, having mixtures of features of both. Furthermore, it is quite common to find people who had the behaviour typical of Kanner's syndrome in early childhood who change with age until, by adolescence, they behave just like someone with Asperger's syndrome (see Chapter 14).

In the latest editions of the ICD and DSM classification systems, Asperger's syndrome is distinguished from other autistic disorders by having no delay in onset of speech and other aspects of the development of adaptive skills. The difficulty with this is that many people who, by adolescence, have the behaviour Asperger described, did have developmental delays, including late speaking.

ICD 10 also includes 'atypical autism' diagnosed on either insufficient features for typical autism, or onset after three years, or both. In DSM IV this would be classified as 'other pervasive developmental disorder'. Parents find these diagnoses unhelpful. Such children present the same disturbances of behaviour and have the same needs as those with typical autism. It is particularly distressing if the label 'atypical' is used as an excuse to exclude a child from appropriate educational services.

ICD 10 and DSM IV also include a diagnosis of 'childhood disintegrative disorder'. In this, development is said to be normal up to two years and then there is loss of skills in at least two of the following areas: language; play; social skills or adaptive behaviour; bowel or bladder control; motor skills. This diagnosis is also a source of confusion. A substantial minority of children with autistic disorders begin to say words around one year and then stop speaking. Some start again later and some do not. Around the time they cease to speak they often become more socially withdrawn and perhaps lose the interest they had in manipulating toys. The vast majority of these children, whether or not they begin to speak again, have clinical pictures that cannot be distinguished from others with autistic disorders who did not show a temporary or permanent loss of skills in their second or third year. The course and prognosis are the same as with other autistic disorders of comparable severity.

The word 'disintegrative' suggests a downhill course and some parents of children given this diagnosis expect the child to become progressively more disabled. Very rarely, this does happen because the child concerned has a physical condition affecting the brain that is progressive. The autistic pattern of behaviour is seen during one stage of this progression. These conditions need to be identified and separated from the usual autistic spectrum disorders. They alone merit the label 'disintegrative'.

Elizabeth Newson described a pattern of behaviour in children that she called 'pathological demand avoidance' (PDA) syndrome. The children concerned have speech but use this to distract their teacher or carer so that they can avoid doing any task. Once again, the problem is that children who have any kind of autistic spectrum disorder can show this type of behaviour.

Some workers are studying whether autistic disorders associated with average or high levels of ability have other specific differences from those associated with varying degrees of generalized learning difficulties. There certainly are differences but it is not clear if they are due only to differing severity of the disabilities or if there are differences in the nature of the impairments underlying the clinical pictures.

Attempts to delineate specific sub-groups of autistic spectrum disorders are confounded by the considerable overlap among the suggested syndromes. The clinical picture of every type of autistic disorder is made up of a large number of features. In clinical practice the more you see of these conditions, the more it appears that any combination of the features is possible. Some combinations are more likely than others but there are no absolute rules. The boundaries are always difficult to define.

For all these reasons, from the point of view of helping the person concerned, spending time on assigning them to a sub-group is of little value. The main clinical task is to decide if they have an autistic spectrum disorder and then to assess their pattern of abilities. The demands of research are different from those of clinical work and investigators may reasonably choose to examine whether specific, separate sub-groups can be found among the autistic spectrum disorders. The important point is to separate the need to help individuals from the demands of research.

The behaviour of children
with autistic spectrum disorders

Each individual with an autistic disorder is different from every other so these descriptions should be taken as a general guide and not as an exact specification for diagnosis. Nevertheless, the common problems affecting social interaction, communication and imagination and the repetitive behaviour can be recognized behind all the variations.

Many, perhaps most, children with autistic disorders show signs of their social and communication problems from early infancy. But, because they cannot move around, the range of behaviour possible for a baby is limited. For this reason, at this stage the signs of the impairments are not obvious and are easily missed by parents. It is not until the child begins to walk independently that the full extent of autistic behaviour can emerge.

Behaviour in babies

Because diagnosis is rarely made before two years of age at the earliest, the details of behaviour in babyhood have been collected from the memories of parents of older children.

Some babies who later show autistic behaviour appear to develop normally for a time and their parents do not notice anything unusual in the first year or so. However, for many, perhaps most of these, careful and systematic questioning shows that there were unusual aspects of behaviour even in the first year. Other babies give their parents cause for concern almost from birth. Sometimes mothers say that they felt something was wrong within the first few days, but they usually cannot tell why they had this feeling. Feeding problems are fairly common and some of the babies do not suck well.

There seem to be three kinds of babies who have autistic disorders. The majority tend to be placid and undemanding, content to lie quietly in their prams all day. Sometimes mothers feel that a child of this kind does not know when he or she is hungry because they do not cry to be fed. In infancy, they are said to be 'angel babies' but parents tend to become concerned as time goes on and the baby does not become more active or sociable. In contrast, a minority scream a great deal both day and night and cannot be comforted or soothed. There are also some babies who are later diagnosed as autistic who fit neither of these descriptions and whose behaviour pattern, viewed retrospectively, seemed to show no unusual features.

The babies may dislike any interference such as nappy changing, dressing and washing. They may not lift their arms or make themselves ready to be picked up. When held they tend not to snuggle down comfortably in their mother's arms and, later on, may not grip with their hands and knees if carried pick-a-back. Some babies are fascinated by lights, or by anything that shines, twinkles or spins. An intense interest in the visual stimuli from the television set may appear very early, as may fascination with music. On the other hand the babies seem uninterested in things that catch the attention of other babies as they grow and develop. Typically, they do not lean out of their prams in eager curiosity to look at people and animals and the passing scene, nor do they try to attract their mother's attention to these things by pointing and making eye contact. A recent study by Simon Baron-Cohen and colleagues has shown that, if this behaviour is absent at 18 months of age, it is very likely indeed that the child is autistic. Some do point to one or a few specific things that interest them but are not concerned to share the enjoyment. Some do not begin to point until long past infancy, if at all. Babies may smile when tickled, cuddled or bounced up and down, but not when looking at someone's face. They may not join in by copying the parents' actions in baby games such as peep-bo or pat-a-cake.

Babies with autistic disorders often smile, cut their teeth, sit up, crawl and walk at the usual ages and gain weight normally, once early feeding problems have passed. Sometimes the motor milestones are delayed, especially in those who later fit Asperger's descriptions or those who have other disabilities affecting motor development. They may not bother to sit up even when able to, apparently because the world is of little interest. A number of the children stand up and walk holding on to the furniture at the right time, but may be reluctant to let go and walk without support until many months after the usual age. There are some stories of young children who crawled or shuffled everywhere until two or more years of age and then suddenly stood up and walked and ran without any previous practice.

Babbling tends to be limited in quantity and poor in quality and usually does not develop the intonation pattern and range of sounds of ordinary speech, which normally begins around the end of the first year.

Behaviour diagnostic of autistic spectrum disorders

For the majority of children with autistic disorders, parents become aware of problems gradually. They often begin to worry in the second year if the child is not talking or if the behaviour pattern is different from that of other children of the same age. If the child has a high level of skill in some areas, parents may not become concerned until the third year or even later. In a minority, development appears to the parents to be proceeding normally, then a marked change in behaviour occurs over a few weeks or months, perhaps with regression in some skills, particularly speech. In both types of onset, the behaviour diagnostic of an autistic spectrum disorder emerges sooner or later in the pre-school years.

I shall start by describing the triad of social, communication and imagination impairments and the repetitive behaviour that are crucial for diagnosis and then go on to the other features that are often seen.

IMPAIRMENTS OF SOCIAL INTERACTION

This is shown in different ways. It is easiest to describe the varieties by grouping them into four main types, although there is no sharp cut-off between them.

i *The aloof group*

This is probably the single most common type of social impairment in young children and is seen most clearly at this stage. In some it continues throughout life, though others do change as they grow older.

Those who are socially aloof behave as though other people did not exist. They do not come when they are called, they do not respond if you speak to them, their faces may be empty of expression except when they experience the extremes of anger, distress or joy, they look through or past you, just occasionally giving you a quick sideways glance, they may pull away if you touch them, they do not put their arms round you if you cuddle them and they may walk past you (or over you, if you are sitting on the floor) without pausing in their stride.

If they want something they cannot reach they grab you by the back of your hand or arm, not placing their hand inside yours or looking up at you, and pull you along to use your hand to reach the object they desire or to carry out an action for them such as turning the handle of a door. Once the object is obtained, you are ignored again.

They show no interest or sympathy if you are in pain or distress. They seem cut off, in a world of their own, completely absorbed in their own aimless activities. However, as children, most of them do respond to rough-and-tumble play. When tickled, swung round, rolled on the floor or chased around they may laugh with delight and show great pleasure. They may even look into your eyes and indicate that they want you to continue. In these situations, the children seem happy and sociable as if nothing is wrong. The moment the game is finished, the child becomes aloof once more.

In childhood, the social impairment is particularly noticeable in contrast to other children of the same age. In normal development, interest in other children is evident very early on, well before school age. Young children with autistic disorders in the aloof group are indifferent to or alarmed by their companions in play group, or nursery school. Even if they will accept their sisters or brothers, they do not interact with children outside the family. The adults who continue to be aloof have no interest in their peers. If they want something, they approach whoever is in charge, though how, despite their social impairments, they unerringly identify the senior person is an unsolved mystery.

ii *The passive group*

This is the least common type of social impairment. These children or adults are not completely cut off from others. They accept social approaches and do not move away from others but they do not initiate social interaction. They may have poor eye contact, like the aloof group, but are more likely to meet other people's gaze when reminded to do so. Because, during childhood, they are amenable and willing to do as they are told, other children are often happy to involve them in their play. A passive child makes an ideal baby in a game of mothers and fathers or a patient in a pretend hospital. The problem is, when the game changes, the passive child may be left behind because there is no suitable role for them.

In general, children and adults of this kind have the least behaviour problems of any with autistic disorders. However, some change markedly in adolescence and become disturbed in behaviour.

iii *The 'active but odd' group*

I first described this group in a paper written in 1979. Ever since then I have tried to think of a name that sounds better but without success. 'Active but odd' describes them precisely and many people now use the term.

Children and adults of this kind make active approaches to other people, usually those in charge rather than their age peers, but do so in a peculiar one-sided fashion to make demands or to go on and on about their own concerns. They pay no attention to the feelings or needs of the people they talk to. Some have poor eye contact but the problem is usually timing of making and breaking eye contact rather than avoidance. They often stare too long and hard when talking to, or rather at, others. Their approaches can include physically holding or hugging the other person, often much too tightly. They can become difficult and aggressive if they are not given the attention they demand. In childhood, they may ignore children of their own age or else behave aggressively towards them.

This group tends to present particular problems of diagnosis because the active social approaches cover up the fact that they have no real understanding of how to interact socially with other people.

iv *The over-formal, stilted group*

This pattern of behaviour is not seen until later adolescence and adult life. It develops in those who are the most able and have a good level of language. They are excessively polite and formal in their behaviour. They try very hard to behave well and cope by sticking rigidly to the rules of social interaction. They do not really understand these rules and have special difficulty with adapting to the subtle differences in behaviour expected in different situations and the changes that occur over time. They can make mistakes because of this lack of true understanding. One young man was as distantly polite to his family as he was to strangers. However, he wished to have a girl friend and, after reading a magazine article about the need to be positive and seize the initiative, he approached a girl he did not know and asked her, very politely, if he could kiss her.

The lack of understanding of other people's thoughts and feelings is evident in all the different sub-groups, even when there is the desire to be kind and helpful.

IMPAIRMENTS OF COMMUNICATION

All children and adults with autistic disorders have problems with *communication*. Their *language* (that is grammar, vocabulary, even the ability to define the meanings of single words) may or may not be impaired. The problem lies with the way they use whatever language they do have.

i *Using speech*

Delay and abnormality in development of speech are very common and Kanner considered them to be an essential part of his syndrome. The difficulties vary in severity. Some children, perhaps one in four or five of all those with autistic spectrum disorders, never speak, but remain mute all their lives. Some of these are able to produce accurate copies of animal or mechanical noises and perhaps a single word once in a blue moon but do not progress beyond this.

The rest do develop speech, though many begin much later than normal. They often start by repeating words spoken by other people, especially the last word or the last few words of a sentence. The exact accent and intonation of the speaker may be copied. The repetition of words may have little meaning for the child and this empty echoing, like a parrot, is called 'echolalia'. Some children repeat words or phrases they have heard in the past and this is called 'delayed echolalia'. Such phrases may be used appropriately in some situations to ask for things they want. Because the child is copying the exact words of the speaker, they reverse the pronouns, for example, asking for a drink by saying 'Do you want juice?' with the intonation of a question because this is what they have heard many times when given a drink.

A child may always use the same phrase or sentence in a particular situation because that was how it was first heard. The association of the phrase with the situation may be completely arbitrary. Kanner gave the example of a boy who said 'Peter eater' whenever he saw anything that looked like a saucepan because his mother had been reciting 'Peter, Peter, pumpkin eater' when she had accidentally dropped a saucepan. This idiosyncratic way of using words sounds very odd to strangers though parents can usually work out the reasons why the child has latched on to the phrase.

Some children never pass the stage of echoed speech but others move on to the next phase, when they begin to say some words and phrases they work out for themselves. At first a child will name things that they want, such as 'sweetie', 'drink', 'ice-cream'. They may then, after months or years, go on to use spontaneous phrases, which may be produced with painful effort, often with mistakes in grammar and word meanings.

As if they are learning a foreign language, the children may find difficulty with the little linking words such as 'in', 'on', 'under', 'before' and 'because'. They may leave them out altogether, saying for example 'want dinner', 'go car shops'. Later on they may put them in sentences but use them wrongly, as in 'put cup in table', 'sit from chair'. One particular mistake the children make is to confuse two words that are opposite in meaning, or else to use one word of the pair for both its true and its opposite meaning. Thus 'switch on light' may be a request to switch the light on or off depending on the circumstances. Often one can see that the child is using the word 'on' to say 'do something appropriate to the light' and that the precise meaning of 'on' and 'off' has not been grasped. Similarly, words that usually occur in pairs can be confused. 'Brush' may be called 'comb', or 'sock' may be called 'shoe'. Even 'Mummy' and 'Daddy' may be misnamed although the child's behaviour clearly shows that they do differentiate between their parents.

Some children retain these abnormalities of speech into adult life. Others improve in their speech and some, sooner or later, develop good grammar and a large vocabulary. Some have apparently normal speech without any early delay, especially those who, as adolescents and adults, fit the description given by Asperger of his syndrome. But, even those who do appear to have normal language have a range of subtle problems. There are some who, despite having a good vocabulary, speak very little. Others talk at length but tend not to use colloquial expressions, so that their speech sounds old-fashioned and pedantic. If asked a question, they give full replies, often providing far more detail than is needed. One young man was asked, in a psychological test, why police were needed. He launched into the history of the police, starting with Sir Robert Peel. Some love dictionaries and encyclopaedias and this is evident in their speech. It has been said that the speech of a person of this kind is similar to that of a computer translating from a foreign language, like the boy who asked his mother, 'May I extract a biscuit from the container?' and another who, after being given a cup of tea, said, 'I wish to thank you for the hospitality you have extended to me this afternoon'.

The content of the speech of those children and adults who can talk is repetitive and not conversational. They may go on and on asking the same questions regardless of the answers or deliver a monologue on their special interests regardless of the response of the audience. Some adults have learnt that such repetitive talking is not socially acceptable and try not to do it but, given the slightest opportunity, they cannot resist returning to their favourite themes.

ii *Understanding speech*

The level of understanding varies as widely as the use of speech. Some children and adults understand no spoken speech and do not respond when spoken to. They may appear to comprehend more than they really do because they use their eyes to pick up clues to situations.

Most do have some understanding. This may be limited to

names of familiar objects or simple instructions in context, such as 'Give me your cup' or 'Come and have your tea'. It can be difficult to know how much understanding there is of the words and how much is guessed from the situation. If the child or adult can be sent out of the room to fetch one or two objects it is more obvious that they comprehend the words. One source of confusion is the lack of flexibility in word meaning. Difficulties can arise if objects have more than one name. One child had learnt that the dog's food was served on 'Candy's plate'. One day she was asked to give Candy her food in her *bowl*. The child looked puzzled for a moment, then put the dog's food into the bowl used for washing the dishes.

It is easy to imagine their problems over words that sound the same but have different meanings. For example, a mother said to her daughter, 'I'll meet you after dinner'. This was heard by her son with an autistic disorder, who then said, 'Have meat for dinner' with an expression of pleasure at having understood something at last. This example also illustrates another problem – that is, the tendency to react to one or two words in a sentence and to ignore the rest. One little girl was asked to 'Bring Mummy the pullover on the chair in your bedroom'. The child trotted upstairs and after several minutes staggered in with the chair.

A major characteristic of people with autistic disorders, however good their language seems to be, is their literal interpretation. One boy was told to 'Dry the teapot on the outside, not the inside' and promptly took it out into the garden to wipe it dry. One has to beware of using sayings such as 'crying your eyes out' or 'have you lost your tongue' because these can be taken at face value and cause distress or even terror. Even people who seem to understand well can make all kinds of mistakes. A man who could travel by himself bought a travel card for the first time. On it was written 'valid for travel until midnight'. He returned home exhausted in the small hours having been travelling on the underground until midnight because he thought the words on the card were an absolute instruction. An invitation to a person with autism to 'call in and see me again when you are passing', which is said merely for politeness, can lead to many unwanted, lengthy visits at inappropriate times. Children with autistic disorders react badly to verbal teasing because, if they have some understanding, they take it seriously. They also have little or no understanding of jokes depending on verbal ambiguity. They may try to tell jokes but do not know why they are funny or else they invent jokes that have no point at all. They know that telling funny stories is what people do but they do not understand why.

The most able people with autistic disorders, by the time they are adults, have a very good understanding and use of complex speech in relation to the subjects that interest them. They can still make elementary mistakes and often seem to understand long, obscure words but be confused by the simplest everyday ones.

iii *Intonation and voice control*

The great majority of people with autistic disorders have odd intonation, which may be monotonous or inappropriate in inflexion. They have problems in controlling the volume of their speech, which may be too loud or, less commonly, too quiet. The voice may have an odd, mechanical, robot-like quality. These difficulties are more obvious with spontaneous than with echoed speech. Improvement may occur with increasing age.

Some occasionally use a 'special' voice, different from their ordinary one. This may be a copy of something they have heard but sometimes seems to be an attempt to try out different sounds. When they do speak, many of the children and adults enunciate words clearly although some have varying degrees of difficulty in this aspect of speech.

iv *Using and understanding non-verbal communication*

Normally, people communicate with each other in many ways other than speaking. They use gestures, facial expressions and bodily movements to accompany speech. In a foreign country they may mime their needs or demonstrate with objects. Deaf people can lip read, or use manual sign language, or write down what they want to say. Children who have a language disorder but who are not autistic communicate in gesture, facial expression and mime. Children and adults with autism are impaired in using even these alternative methods of communication.

Before they develop speech, most show their needs by grabbing someone by the hand, pulling them along and putting their hand on the desired object. It may be years before the children begin to point and then they usually begin by using their whole hand rather than pointing with one finger. Only a very few attempt to mime their needs and the movements tend to be as brief and sketchy as possible.

Simple gestures such as nodding and shaking of the head to mean yes or no do develop in many of the children but more complex gestures are rare. Some adults do reach the stage of waving their arms around when speaking, but these movements tend to bear no relation to what is being said.

Attempts are often made to teach manual sign language, such as Makaton, to children and adults with little or no communication. Some will copy signs but never use them spontaneously. Others use them but show the characteristic autistic abnormalities equivalent to those found in speech. A few do become able to use this method of communicating effectively. Despite the limitations, teaching manual signs can be helpful for people who have no other way to express their needs.

Young children with autistic disorders have as much trouble in understanding non-verbal communication as in using it. As time goes on, however, they begin to have some comprehension of the meaning of clear, simple gestures and expressions. They may then appear to understand more of what is said than they really do, because they find clues in people's movements as well as the general context in which communication occurs.

IMPAIRMENTS OF IMAGINATION

Children with autistic disorders do not develop pretend play and imaginative activities in the same way as other children. Many never have any kind of pretend play. They handle toys and other objects purely for physical sensations. Some reach the stage of using objects, including miniature toys, for their obvious purposes, such as sweeping with a toy broom or moving trains along a track. A number can perform some quite complex play sequences of this kind but do not act out imaginative stories.

Some of the more able children do show more evidence of what seems like imagination. They act out a sequence of events that they have invented. This looks convincing at first but prolonged observation shows that the child goes through the same sequence over and over again, without any changes. Most do not involve other children but, if they do, they usually want the others to take part in the same repetitive activity. They do not join in other children's imaginative games. They may reach a stage when they want to take part but do not know how.

Another type of behaviour engaged in by some children that appears to be imaginative is the enacting of a character, sometimes copied from television or a book, sometimes an animal or bird or even an inanimate object such as a railway engine. The actions are limited and repetitive, not inventive. The curious feature of this behaviour is that the child seems to be living the character or object, rather than pretending.

Many like television and videos but the most popular types of videos and television shows are cartoons, such as Thomas the Tank Engine, quiz shows with lots of clapping, mechanical noises and flashing lights, science-fiction and films with a lot of action. Soap operas are liked by some because of their familiar characters. Those children who do like to hear stories read to them or recorded on audio-tape want the same ones over and over again. They know if any word is missed out. They do not have an imaginative understanding of the story although they may be able to repeat whole chunks word for word.

The pleasures of creative imagination in childhood are denied to autistic people and so are the rewards in adult life. They have limited or no understanding of other people's emotions, so find it hard to share happiness or sorrow. They are impaired in the ability to share ideas with others and to use past and present experiences to plan for the future. Most of the usual sources of satisfaction are a closed book to people with autism. They find their pleasures in their own special interests.

REPETITIVE STEREOTYPED ACTIVITIES

This aspect of autistic behaviour makes most sense if seen as the other side of the coin of impairment of imagination. If the person with autism cannot enjoy the activities that involve flexible, creative thinking, cannot enjoy exchanging ideas with other people, has no understanding of or interest in other people and cannot integrate past and present experiences to make plans for the future, the only thing left is the reassurance of repeating those activities that do give some pleasure.

i *Simple repetitive activities*

The simplest forms of these activities involve repetitive sensations. Tasting, smelling, feeling or tapping and scratching different surfaces, listening to mechanical noises, staring at lights or shiny things, twisting and turning hands or objects near the eyes, staring at things from different angles, switching lights on and off, watching things spinning round or self-spinning, are all examples of behaviour seen in people with autistic disorders. Sometimes the repetitive activity takes the form of self-biting, head banging, hitting, scratching or other forms of self-injury. More often, behaviour of this kind is a response to distress, anger or frustration but self-injury can be a repetitive habit in someone who has no other way of occupying themselves.

The simple repetitive activities occur mostly in young children. They tend to continue longer in those with the most severe generalized disabilities and may last into adult life.

ii *Elaborate repetitive routines*

These routines are found especially in children with autism as described by Kanner. There are many variations in the way the pattern is shown.

Some have routines that they invent for themselves, such as tapping on their chair before sitting down, standing up and turning round three times in the course of a meal or carrying out a complex sequence of bodily movements. Placing objects in long lines that must not be disturbed is a familiar feature of autistic behaviour. In older children and adults this can take the form of a rigid arrangement of their possessions, which no one must disturb, however much dust accumulates.

In other cases the routines derive from an activity initiated usually by the parents, which, having once been done in a certain way, must continue without change. One child always wanted the same route for her daily walk, another insisted that the whole family kept to the same places at the table for every meal. A little boy, in the days before central heating became common, would watch intently as his mother laid the fire and became extremely upset if she did not place the paper, wood and coal in precisely the same pattern every day. Another insisted on a lengthy bedtime routine ending with him lying in the exact centre of his bed while his parents arranged the blankets and eiderdown in a special way, without any creases. Typically, if the routine is upset there are screams and temper tantrums that can be ended only by starting the routine from the beginning again.

The children may become attached to certain objects and refuse to be parted from them. These may be ordinary toys like dolls or teddy bears, but often they are oddments such as pieces of string, holly leaves, tiny squares of photographic negative, little bits of concrete, or pieces of brightly coloured plastic. Some children are collectors of such domestic items as empty detergent packets, tins, plastic bottles, or dustpans. They will go to any lengths to add to their store. One little boy, when he realized he had to wait till detergent packets were empty, would throw away the powder from a full packet if it was left in his reach. Another child used to take tins of furniture polish from displays in super-markets and would even run into people's houses to find such tins if he had the opportunity. He always knew exactly where to look in any house and could run in, grab a polish tin and run out before the house owner realized anything had happened.

Resistance to change can apply to food. Though some children have good appetites from the beginning, others go through a stage in which they refuse to eat more than a few items.

Repetitive acting out of characters and sequences from tele-vision series has become fairly common among the children since video recorders have been generally available. Batman, the Incredible Hulk and the Daleks have all been copied in their day. Currently, Thomas the Tank Engine is the most popular obsession. It appears that the children are fascinated by the bizarre, mechanical and repetitive characteristics of the charac-ters they copy. Watching video recordings has had a marked effect on the behaviour of children with autistic disorders prob-ably because a video repeats the same events every time it is shown without the slightest variation – the ideal entertainment for the person with autism. Many of the children and adults who are fascinated with certain videos replay the same short sequences so often that the tape breaks.

Music can be the focus of a repetitive routine. Most autistic people are fascinated by music and may play the same tunes on records, cassettes or compact discs over and over again. They may know one conductor's interpretation of a piece and object strongly if they hear another's rendering. Television commercials that combine music and visual stimuli can also become a special interest even if no other programmes are watched.

The behaviours described above are most often seen in child-hood though they can continue into adult life.

In more able children, especially those with the behaviour known as Asperger's syndrome, the elaborate repetitive activities often take the form of fascination with special subjects, such as railway timetables, dinosaurs, the weather, astronomy, science-fiction characters and so on *ad infinitum*. The interest is generally in collecting, memorizing and talking about the facts related to the subjects. For some, there is a special fascination with violence, destruction and death, which can sometimes be combined with high anxiety about these subjects.

The special interest may centre round numbers, numerical aspects of objects or complicated calculations. The routines may be complex, as with the young man who could ride a bicycle and insisted on riding to a new town each weekend in strict alphabetical order according to the initial of the name. As he lived in the USA, he had a fair chance of finding towns beginning with the more unusual letters.

This type of complex repetitive behaviour often lasts into adult life.

Other features of behaviour

These behaviours are common but by no means universal and are not crucial for diagnosis.

MOVEMENTS

i *Stereotyped movements*

These movements, often referred to as 'stereotypies', occur in most children with autistic disorders and often continue into adult life. They include finger flicking, flapping arms and hands, jumping up and down, head rolling, rocking while standing up, often springing from back to front foot and making facial grimaces. Many walk on tiptoe, with an odd springy gait.

These movements of hands, limbs and face are most obvious when the child or adult is excited, agitated or angry or is gazing at something that has absorbed their whole attention, such as a spinning object. On the other hand, if they are occupied in some constructive activity, the movements may be minimal or absent.

The reasons for these stereotyped movements are not known for certain. Some could be classified as simple repetitive activities, carried out in order to obtain sensations but others seem to be the result of generalized excitation of the whole body. Body movements with excitement, including arm flapping, are normal in all babies and toddlers. With increasing age there is usually increasing control over such movements but people with autistic disorders appear to remain immature in this respect. They can become tense and distressed if made to suppress their odd movements for long periods of time.

ii *Abnormalities of gait and posture*

Some children with autistic disorders, especially those who fit Kanner's descriptions, are agile climbers and are able to walk along narrow ledges with perfect balance and without fear. Other children, especially those with the behaviour described by Asperger, appear clumsy and may be fearful of climbing. Nearly all the children are immature in the way they move. They may not swing their arms appropriately when walking and may walk with head and shoulders bent forward. They may run clumsily with arms outstretched. They may climb or descend stairs standing on each step in turn when they are old enough to alternate their feet. Many of the children have odd postures. They may hold their arms, hands and fingers stretched out or bent at peculiar angles. The abnormalities of gait and posture become more noticeable with increasing age and are most obvious in adolescence and adult life.

Children and adults may be skilful and nimble with their fingers, or they may have poor fine finger co-ordination. They tend to do things they want to do with speed and dexterity but have limp or clumsy movements when asked to do things that do not interest them.

Some of the children have difficulty with learning to chew lumpy food, probably because of the difficulties of co-ordinating the muscles involved in chewing and swallowing and have to have their food mashed up for them for considerably longer than normal.

Most children and adults with autism have marked problems with physical education and games. Many of them acquire physical skills they can pursue individually, such as swimming, horse-riding and trampolining. The problems arise in team games when they have to co-ordinate their movements with those of several others as well as remembering the rules. The planning and organizing involved defeats almost all people with autistic disorders, although there is a small minority with skill in one or two team games.

iii *Imitating movements*

Imitation of other people's actions, including facial expressions, should begin in the first year of life. Children with autism typically are delayed in imitating and those most severely affected never do so. It is paradoxical that echoing other people's words is so common, while there are so many problems in copying movements. Parents often find that they have to teach their child with autism to wave, to play baby games and to perform action songs by moving the child's limbs until the action is acquired. All kinds of skills may have to be taught this way because of the lack of any drive to copy others. Some who do begin to imitate, copy other people's actions precisely but meaninglessly. This is known as 'echopraxia', a word that is similar to 'echolalia', that is, echoing of speech. Imitation is one of the skills that is basic to developing social behaviour, so its impairment is a significant part of the autistic picture.

RESPONSES TO SENSORY STIMULATION

i *Responses to sounds*

Young children with autistic conditions may be thought to be deaf because they tend not to respond when spoken to and may ignore very loud sounds. They may even fail to blink if someone drops a pile of plates behind them. Parents usually suspect that their child can hear because they notice that he or she responds immediately to some sounds, such as a favourite television commercial jingle, or the sound of chocolate being unwrapped. In his report of 1801, Itard wrote about Victor, the Wild Boy of Aveyron, 'Of all his senses the ear appeared the least sensitive. It was found, nevertheless, that the sound of a cracking walnut or other favourite eatable never failed to make him turn round ... yet this same organ showed itself insensible to the loudest noises and the explosion of firearms.'

A child may be fascinated by some sounds such as that made by friction drive toys or the ringing of a bell. They may find some sounds intensely distressing and will cover their ears and cringe away from, for example, the roar of a motor bike or the barking of a dog or even some comparatively quiet sounds, though they never seem to be sensitive to the noises they make themselves. Ignoring some sounds, fascination with others and distress at yet others may all occur in the same individual.

These odd responses to sounds, especially the oversensitivity, tend to become less marked with increasing age and may eventually disappear.

ii *Responses to visual stimuli*

People with autism, especially children, can show the same tendency to be fascinated by, to ignore or to be distressed by visual stimuli as they do to sounds. On the whole, the response of fascination with bright lights is the most common, though some can be overly distressed by, for example, photographic flash lights.

When young, some of the children may look at something that moves but lose interest when the movement stops. They seem to recognize people and objects by their general outline rather than by details of their appearance. This suggests that the children may make most use of the peripheral part of the retina that attends to movement and outline, rather than using the central vision for details. Normally, the movement-detecting part of the eye is used mostly in conditions of near darkness, when it is not possible to observe any detail. It is interesting that some of the young children walk, run and even ride a tricycle without seeming to look where they are going and may find their way in the dark quite as easily as in the light. Some young autistic children may not bother to switch on the light if alone in a dark room but can find their own possessions and move around with no difficulty.

These unusual features of response to visual stimuli tend to fade with increasing age.

iii *Responses to proximal sensations*

This term refers to touch, taste, smell, vibration, pain and temperature, all of which involve direct bodily contact, as distinct from the 'distance' senses of hearing and vision. Again, the response can be fascination, distress or indifference. The children seem to explore the world through these senses for much longer than usual. They may touch and lick and smell people as well as objects.

Some children show evident dislike of being touched and will pull away even from gentle, affectionate touches. A few are over-sensitive to smells and complain at even faint odours. The feeling of clothing, especially shoes and socks, is disliked by some children. Temple Grandin, a very able adult with autism, in her book, *Emergence: Labelled Autistic*, wrote that, when she was a child, a starched petticoat felt to her as if she were wearing barbed wire. This is probably why some of the young children remove their clothes or at least their shoes and socks whenever they can.

Paradoxically, many of the young children are seemingly indifferent to heat or cold and will want to continue with winter clothes in the summer or run out with little or nothing on in icy weather. One of the most surprising features of autism is the indifference to pain. There are many stories of children with broken bones, dental abscesses, appendicitis or other sources of severe pain who make no complaint and behave as if nothing were amiss. They usually do not come for comfort if they hurt themselves. This obliviousness to pain is seen in those with repetitive self-injury.

As with other abnormalities in response to sensory stimuli, these tend to become less marked with age. A child who ignored pain when young may become oversensitive in later childhood and make an enormous fuss at the smallest scratch.

iv *Appetite and thirst*

ʌ As already mentioned, insistence on eating only a small range of foods is one form of resistance to change. The child concerned may have a good appetite for the foods they will eat but a few of the children eat very little and, in rare cases, a child will refuse all food. No-one knows the reason for this but it does seem as if the child does not recognize the meaning of the sensation of hunger.

Much more common is excessive drinking of water, fruit juice, tea or other fluids. This can be a major problem if the intake of fluid is so excessive that it leads to vomiting. Thirst does not seem to be the explanation because, when they are involved in activities they enjoy, the desire to drink seems to be forgotten.

ANXIETY AND SPECIAL FEARS

There are some people with autism who appear to have a high level of anxiety most or all of the time. It has been suggested that autistic behaviour is the result of severe anxiety from early childhood. This explanation is not convincing because, among many other reasons, most children and adults with autistic disorders are not generally anxious. Their anxiety arises in situations they cannot understand and therefore find confusing and distressing. Furthermore, individuals with autism often do not understand real dangers and are calm when others would be anxious. A family about to go by air to a holiday destination, on the night before their flight, saw with some alarm pictures of an air crash on television. Their daughter, who was autistic, loved watching repairs of broken objects, so her response to the sight of the crashed aeroplane was the comment, 'Man come and mend it' said with happy expectation. A boy liked the sound of squealing car brakes and would dash in front of cars to make them brake sharply and thus produce this, to him, delightful noise.

It is quite common for the children to develop specific fears of harmless things, such as balloons, dogs, being bathed, riding in buses, even a particular colour or shape. These fears can last for years and may create difficulties for the whole family, especially if they are of common everyday objects or events that can hardly be avoided.

ATTENTION AND MOTIVATION

Typically, in autistic disorders, attention span is good for activities that interest the child. It may be sustained for a length of time that is surprising, given the age of the child. In contrast, attention for activities or tasks that are outside the range of interests is much shorter and may be fleeting or non-existent. Given supervision, attention may be held for longer but tends to cease once the guidance is withdrawn. If there are very severe or profound learning difficulties, there may be no special interests and no sustained attention to anything.

The root of the problem in those with good attention when they choose is lack of motivation to engage in anything outside the special interests. For example, there is usually little or no drive to become independent, so the child, or even adult, is quite happy to allow a parent or carer to dress, wash, even feed them. Left to themselves, children and many adults with autistic disorders are distracted from these self-care tasks by stimuli or activities that fascinate them. As a result, they are so slow in completing the tasks that parents take over when there is a need to hurry. For this reason, parents are often accused of impeding the child's development of independence. The truth is that the demands of ordinary family life make it very difficult to encourage the growth of independence if the children have no interest in doing things for themselves.

SPECIAL SKILLS

Typically, in autistic spectrum disorders, there are marked differences in the levels of ability on psychological tests of different kinds of skills. Most often, visuo-spatial skills that do not involve language, like completing jigsaw puzzles, matching shapes and so on, are performed better than skills that do need language. A minority do better on verbal tests but these are of the kind that need a good rote memory rather than understanding of abstract ideas or social rules. Since there are exceptions to everything, a few people perform more or less equally on all tests.

Perhaps one in 10 individuals with autistic spectrum disorders have certain specific skills in which they excel, even in comparison with the normal population. Sometimes the people concerned are of more or less average ability in other areas but there are some individuals who have severe learning difficulties apart from their isolated skills.

The special abilities that have been reported include playing a musical instrument or even composing music; performing lengthy numerical calculations such as extracting square roots from huge numbers; identifying the days of the week on which any date fell or will fall in a wide span of years; reading fluently at a very young age though comprehension of the text is poor; memorizing huge quantities of facts about favourite subjects; assembling constructional toys or mechanical or electrical apparatus; working with computers. Some, like Stephen Wiltshire, have remarkable ability with regard to drawing. The skills depend upon visuo-spatial abilities and/or rote memory. For example, those who draw well remember and reproduce things they have seen. They may, like Nadia when she was young, be able to rotate mentally something they have seen and draw it from another point of view. It is remarkable that the gifted artists with autistic disorders draw accurately in perspective from a very young age, unlike other young children who go through many stages before grasping the rules of perspective. Sometimes they will draw only in one medium. Nadia drew with a blue ball-point pen, or on steam on a window. With crayons, for example, her drawings were childish. These skills tend to become a focus for the repetitive routines. Thus the drawings are of the same subjects, the music is played repetitively, the calendar calculators want to be fed dates all the time.

Some of those with special skills at some time in childhood or adult life cease using them. The reason for this is unknown, nor is it clear whether the skills are lost or just no longer used. They are rarely taken up again despite any amount of encouragement. Nadia stopped her remarkable drawings when her speech developed but there is no general evidence that speech and visuo-spatial skills are incompatible. Stephen Wiltshire is able to speak as well as to draw.

INAPPROPRIATE BEHAVIOUR

Inappropriate, difficult behaviour is frequent in children with autistic disorders. The causes include confusion and fear of unfamiliar situations; interference with repetitive routines; failure to understand social rules; inappropriate attempts to control events; oversensitivity to sensory input from loud sounds, bright lights, crowds of people; pursuit of preferred activities without any ability to consider the consequences.

In the family home, the children can be restless, destructive, noisy, aggressive if frustrated and given to running away if the opportunity occurs. They may sleep very little and disturb the family when awake. Their demands and their routines may eventually take priority over all the family's other needs because of the severity of the temper tantrums if the child is thwarted in any way.

Often, behaviour in public is as difficult as it is at home. The children who are given to screaming are not inhibited by being in a public place and will scream as loud and long in the street as at home. They may take things off shop counters, run round the aisles of supermarkets, lie on the floor in a temper tantrum or run into the street regardless of traffic. The young children have no idea that it is not done to take off one's clothes in public and may happily disrobe to sit in an inviting puddle of rain water, if so inclined. They may touch the hair, clothing, wristwatch or other possessions of strangers, ignoring any protests. The problems may be so severe that the parents cannot take the child with them when they shop and holidays away from home are impossible.

The children who have good language may be more amenable but they can cause small social crises. They do not understand that some things are better left unsaid. They may talk about topics that are not mentioned in polite society. Innocently, they make inappropriate remarks. All young children are liable to be tactless but the tendency is more marked and goes on to a much later age in children who are autistic. One girl of 12 years, who spoke very well, on seeing an unusually short woman, said, in her loud, clear voice, 'Mummy, look at that dear little lady'. A child, looking at a new born infant, commented to the proud mother, 'What an awful face'. Most people with autism, even those with good speech, never tell lies. They do not understand why it should ever be necessary to avoid the truth and in any case lack the skill with language and ideas needed to invent lies. If they do reach the stage of telling lies this is done without any subtlety and is easily detected. Some tell fantastic stories on their favourite themes but these are not motivated by the desire to deceive. The sources of such stories are usually easily recognized and tend to be based on television, books, or films.

The social naivety can lead to inappropriately friendly approaches to strangers. Parents of the more able adolescents worry about the possible dangers in this behaviour and feel they have to restrict their child's freedom on this account.

Just like young normal children, children with autistic disorders tend to pick up bad language and terms of abuse. Unlike normal children they are unaware of the need for discretion and may use swear words on most unsuitable occasions.

People outside the family may blame the parents for 'spoiling' their child but no-one who has not had direct experience can know what it is like to live with a child of this kind. Children with autistic conditions are totally egocentric, not because of deliberate selfishness but because they have no concept that others have thoughts or feelings. They lack any desire to please and most have no anxiety about parental displeasure. The usual ways of interacting with children and teaching them social rules do not apply in this situation. However, there are ways of helping to make behaviour more appropriate, as will be discussed in Chapter 10.

Epileptic fits

Fits cannot, strictly speaking, be classified as 'behaviour' but they are included in this description because they are a commonly occurring part of the clinical picture.

Among the children who have learning difficulties as well as autistic disorders, about one quarter to one third have had at least one epileptic fit by the time they are reach adult life. Fits can occur in those of average or higher levels of ability but are much less common. They may begin in infancy, childhood, adolescence, or even in adult life. In some, the fits occur only with a fever. Some teenagers may have one or two and then no more. Other children or adolescents have recurrent fits for many years or all their lives. Any type of fit may be seen among those with autistic disorders.

Changes with growing up

Autistic behaviour tends to be most obvious to the parents and most typical in the years from two to five. The exception to this occurs among the most able children with little or no delay in language development. Their parents may attribute their lack of interest in other children and their determination to go their own way as evidence of a strong character and high intelligence. Problems in this group typically become recognized when they start school, refuse to fit into the classroom or playground activities and appear indifferent to any rewards or sanctions.

In children who have shown marked autistic behaviour in their early years, changes often occur around five to six years. In some children, the autistic behaviour becomes much less obvious.

There are children who seem to lose all the typical abnormalities apart from a few subtle signs in their social relationships. For some, the clinical picture becomes that of a pure developmental language disorder with few if any autistic features. In the majority, the autistic behaviour remains clearly present although, in most, varying degrees of improvement in skills and behaviour occur.

As for all children, adolescence is another time of change. Some go through this stage of life without any special problems and may even improve markedly. In others, there is a return of the temper tantrums, aggression or other inappropriate behaviour seen in the early years.

By adult life, the variations in the ways in which autistic behaviour is manifested become even wider. The most disabled are completely dependent on others and still show the autistic characteristics seen in childhood. At the other end of the scale, the most able are living and working independently and some are married with children. The problems that remain are the subtle impairments of social interaction and communication, though some compensate for these by studying and following the example of other people. In some people, the picture is complicated by a psychiatric illness (see Chapter 14).

Follow-up studies have shown that the most important factor in deciding the amount of intellectual progress is the overall level of ability, which can be measured in childhood by psychological tests of language and visuo-spatial skills as long as these are given by people with skill and experience. These are most likely to be reliable guides if the child is tested after five years of age. The education and care experienced during childhood can affect *behaviour* and can help the child to develop potential skills more quickly, but do not seem to make a significant difference to the final level. In addition to these factors, the individuals most likely to become independent are those with an equable temperament, who have special skills and interests that can be used for paid employment and who have a strong desire to succeed in the world.

·5·

How many children have
autistic spectrum disorders?

Prevalence

All the studies concerning the numbers of people with autistic disorders have counted children and adolescents but, so far, have not included adults. The studies have been of *prevalence* – that is, the number of those in the specified age range living in the specified geographical area at the time the count was made. The term *incidence* is sometimes used but this should properly refer only to the number of *new* cases in a specified time. For autistic disorders, this might be the number of new cases in one year. This would be very difficult to count because of the impossibility at present of making a diagnosis at birth. However, a recent study of children aged 18 months has given some indication of incidence and rough calculations of incidence can be made from the estimates of prevalence.

There have been a number of studies of the prevalence of autism. To determine prevalence it is necessary to count the numbers of people fitting the criteria chosen who live in a defined geographical area. Ideally, the research workers should see everyone in the age range chosen and make their own diagnoses because in many people the presence of an autistic condition has never been recognized. Studies of this kind are called 'epidemiological'. The findings of such studies that have been completed vary from around two to three up to 16 in 10,000. The wide differences are probably due to the definitions of autism used. A few studies have strictly applied Kanner's criteria of severe lack of affective contact (social aloofness) and insistence on elaborate repetitive routines and they found four to five children in every 10,000 in studies carried out in the UK and Denmark in the 1960s and 70s.

The study in Camberwell carried out by Judith Gould and myself in the 1970s (mentioned before in Chapter 1) counted numbers of children using the wide definition of autistic spectrum disorders – that is, all those with the triad of impairments. We included children who had the triad even if they had other conditions as well. Almost all had mild, moderate or severe learning difficulties. We concentrated on these because early studies of Kanner's autism had shown that most had some degree of difficulty with learning. We found about 22 in every 10,000 children had the triad, including those with Kanner's autism. In 1986 Gillberg and his colleagues in Sweden reported similar numbers.

In 1991, the same group of workers in Sweden examined children aged seven to 16 years in mainstream schools in order to find those who fitted Asperger's descriptions – that is, having the triad of impairments in more subtle form than in Kanner's syndrome (see Chapters 1 and 14). They estimated that at least 36 in 10,000 children had Asperger's syndrome. This brings the grand total of all autistic spectrum disorders to at least 58 per 10,000 – almost 6 in every 1000.

Are the numbers increasing?

This question is frequently asked by professionals working with children. Many feel sure that they are seeing more children with autistic disorders than they did in the past.

It is impossible at the moment to give a definite answer. The increase may be apparent rather than real, first, because the definition of autism has been widened from that originally suggested by Kanner, second, because those who see children with developmental disorders have become more aware of autistic conditions in recent years. In particular, the concept of Asperger's syndrome has aroused much interest. It may also be the case that, years ago, many young children with strange and difficult behaviour were placed in the old mental handicap hospitals. Now that there has been a change to community rather than institutional care, the children are being referred to paediatricians and other professionals, who are for this reason seeing more of this type of child.

On the other hand, there may be a real increase in incidence and, in consequence, in prevalence. The evidence to prove or disprove this is not available. If it were possible to do a series of studies from now on, they might show that numbers are still rising, or that they fluctuate from time to time or place to place, but there is no way of finding out what has happened in the past. If there is a marked rise, the reasons are unknown. Explanations such as the effects of pollution, additives in the diet, or the evils of the urban environment have all been suggested but there is no evidence for any of these theories.

Age of onset

Kanner at first believed that his syndrome was always present from birth so he named it 'early infantile autism'. Later, he observed the same syndrome in children who appeared to have had a year or two of normal development before becoming autistic. As previously noted, the ICD 10 and DSM IV criteria specify onset before three years for typical autism. Onset of the behavioural pattern after this age is referred to in these systems as 'atypical autism'.

There can be problems in sorting out the age at which autistic behaviour first appeared. Parents may not realize that their child's behaviour is unusual until the second or third year. At this time they may begin to worry because their child is slow in talking and shows intense resistance to change. Careful questioning usually shows that problems were present from birth or early infancy (see Chapter 4) but, occasionally, there does seem to have been a period of normal development and then a real change to autistic behaviour. This is typically in the second or third year but may be later.

Sometimes this follows a fever, perhaps due to encephalitis (a virus infection of the brain) or some kind of trauma, but there may be no apparent reason. It can follow an event such as a house move or the birth of a sibling. Enough is now known about the essentially physical causes of autistic disorders to suggest that such psychological stresses affect children who were vulnerable and would have developed autistic behaviour in any case.

The latest ICD and DSM criteria for Asperger's syndrome specify normal development in speech and adaptive skills before three years (see Chapter 3) but this conflicts with diagnoses based on the behaviour pattern alone. Specifying ages of onset as essential criteria for diagnosis causes all sorts of problems. The evidence is all based on parents' memories of the early years, unless the child is seen and assessed while very young. Parents can usually describe behaviour but are less accurate in dating events. If the parents are not available, for example, when trying to assess someone seen for the first time as an adult, diagnosis is theoretically impossible. It is better to diagnose on the overall pattern as revealed in the history, rather than on an arbitrary cut-off point based on age.

Numbers of boys compared with girls

Boys are affected more often than girls. Kanner found four times as many boys among children with his autistic syndrome. Asperger at first thought that girls were never affected with his syndrome but later changed his mind. The Swedish study of Asperger's syndrome in mainstream schools found a ratio of four boys to one girl.

There is some evidence that, although girls have autistic disorders less often than boys, when they are affected they are likely to be more severely disabled. The excess of boys is most obvious among those of high ability and becomes smaller the lower the levels of overall intelligence. There are some very able women with autistic disorders but far fewer than men. However, the study in Sweden also identified a group who had some but not all of the criteria for Asperger's syndrome. Including these changed the ratio to 2.3 boys to one girl, suggesting that autistic disorders may be more difficult to recognize in girls.

As with so many aspects of autistic disorders, the reasons for the sex differences are unknown. Perhaps the social instincts of girls are stronger than those of boys so it takes more severe damage to impair them in a girl. Asperger was brave enough to suggest that his syndrome was the extreme end of the continuum of the normal male personality. Solving this question may have relevance to many issues of gender differences.

Parents' occupations

Almost all the autistic children seen by Kanner had fathers who were of higher intelligence and educational level than the average and most had professional occupations. He believed that this was a special feature of autism. Many of the earlier studies of children with Kanner's autism seen at various centres found the same tendency in the parents' occupations, though never to the same marked extent as that described by Kanner. Any sample based on a clinic may be biased by special selection factors. It is probable that parents with professional qualifications were more likely to have heard of Kanner's work and to have had the determination and the means to attend his clinic.

In order to examine this question properly, it is necessary to look at the results of studies that identified all children with autism in a specified area, regardless of whether they had been referred to a special clinic. Out of 16 such studies in Europe, the USA, Canada and Japan, nine gave information on parents' occupations. In only two of these was any bias towards higher class reported and in neither was it anywhere near as large as Kanner had found. It no longer seems likely that autistic disorders occur more often in parents of higher occupational status, though studies specifically concerned with the most able group, especially those who have the behaviour pattern described by Asperger, have not yet been carried out.

·6·

Conditions associated with
autistic spectrum disorders
or autistic-like behaviour

Autistic disorders are problems of aspects of development, so many of the typical features of behaviour are due to extreme immaturity and appear peculiar only because they are discrepant with the age of the individual and in comparison with levels of skill in other areas.

Everything that a child with an autistic disorder does, other children may do at some time or other during their development. Young children who are developing normally can flap their arms with excitement, jump and run round in circles in play. The age when children begin to talk is variable. Children have temper tantrums; they may hold on to a piece of cloth or a teddy bear and weep when it is lost; specific fears are common and so are food fads. With growing independence, especially in the second year, young children can be very uncooperative and inclined to ignore instructions and to say no to every suggestion.

The difference is that in a child whose social development is progressing along normal lines these things happen in passing phases, whereas they continue for years on end in children with autistic disorders. Children who are not autistic, when they reach the appropriate stage of development, normally in the second year, begin to have imaginative play and varied activities, whereas children with autistic disorders are limited and repetitive in the things they do. Most important of all, children who are not autistic have a strong drive to take part in social interaction, communication and play, especially with their age peers.

When making a diagnosis and considering whether developmental disorders other than autism are present, it is important to be aware that autistic spectrum disorders can occur together with any other disability, physical or psychological. If the triad of impairments of social interaction, communication and imagination is present then an autistic disorder should be diagnosed regardless of any other co-existing condition. The triad cannot be explained away by another disability. The question must always be 'Does this child have an autistic disorder *and* (not or) some other condition?' The importance of recognizing the autistic disorder, if present, is that this is the major factor in determining the type of care and education needed by the child, whatever other condition they might have.

Generalized learning difficulties

Learning difficulties and autistic disorders often but by no means always occur together. In autistic disorders specific aspects of the skills needed for adapting to social life are always impaired. However, other abilities may or may not be affected at least as far as obtaining scores on psychological tests of intelligence is concerned. Autistic disorders can be found at any level of ability from profoundly disabled up to average or higher.

Considering the whole range of autistic disorders, including the type described by Asperger, about one third have learning difficulties, the majority of these being severely or profoundly learning-disabled. Most of those in the Asperger group have test scores in the low average range or better. Of those with autism like that described by Kanner, about one third have severe to moderate learning difficulties, one third have mild difficulties and one third are in the low average or better range. Conversely, 50 to 60 per cent of all children with severe or profound learning difficulties also have the triad of impairments but the proportion is very much lower, at around 0.2 to 0.4 per cent, among those with mild learning difficulties or average and above ability.

Among children or adults with severe learning difficulties, there are some who function at such a low level that they have not reached the stages of development at which language and pretend play emerge. Their activities tend to be repetitive and many have stereotyped movements. Diagnosis has to be based on social responsiveness as shown in facial expression, eye contact and bodily movements. At this level, autistic disorder is just one of many problems. However, recognizing that an autistic disorder is present helps parents and other carers to understand that the lack of social responsiveness is not related to any fault in the love and care being given. They can also be aware of the types of stimuli, such as loud sounds, that might cause distress and the activities, such as a sensory room, that might be enjoyed.

Is generalized learning disability part of the autistic disorder or is it due to additional brain dysfunction, perhaps produced by the same original cause as the autism but with a different site for the brain pathology? The facts to answer this question are not yet known. It is most likely that both situations can occur. Autistic disorders adversely affect the ability to learn from social interaction and to make sense out of experiences and this must reduce the capacity to learn and make use of information. The children and adults who score well on tests mostly do so on the strength of their good rote memories and their visuo-spatial not their verbal reasoning abilities. On the other hand, some of the medical conditions associated with autism do give rise to pathological changes in various parts of the brain of which some may be relevant to autistic disorders and others to learning difficulties.

Whatever the causes of the association between autistic disorders and generalized learning difficulties, it is important to consider both separately when making a diagnosis. The presence of one does not explain away the presence of the other.

Rett's syndrome

This is a very rare syndrome so far reported only in girls. After a few months of apparently normal development, the child gradually loses the ability to use her hands to hold and manipulate objects. Repetitive movements of the hands occur, mainly hand wringing or rubbing or tapping both hands together. Head growth slows or stops. Walking is very poor and the child may sooner or later have to use a wheelchair. Curvature of the spine may develop. Over-breathing, air-swallowing and teeth-grinding are common. With the onset of these problems, the child often shows signs of anxiety and becomes socially cut off. There is very severe learning disability, little or no language development and no pretend play. The picture at this stage is like that of an autistic disorder in a very severely disabled child. It is interesting that, over a varying length of time, the children often lose the autistic social impairment and become responsive to social approaches, though retaining all the other features of the syndrome. The cause is unknown, as is the reason for the improvement in sociability.

Fragile X syndrome

This is an inherited condition due to an abnormality of the X chromosome. It is commoner and more marked in males. Certain physical abnormalities, including large ears and a long face, occur in differing degrees of severity. Learning difficulties of varying levels, motor stereotypies, oversensitivity to sound and to touch, repetitive routines and abnormalities of speech are part of the usual picture. Hyperactivity and poor attention span may be seen in the children. The social behaviour is of particular interest. Eye contact is usually avoided and the affected individuals tend to keep a physical distance from other people. However, their social difficulties appear to arise from shyness, anxiety and dislike of being touched rather than from social aloofness and indifference. The quality is different from that in an autistic condition. In a few cases, the autistic type of social impairment occurs. These account for only a small proportion of all people with autistic disorders but chromosome examination for Fragile X is now a standard part of the investigation of autistic behaviour.

Landau-Kleffner syndrome

This very rare disorder occurs in children, usually between three and seven years of age, whose development was previously normal, although some have delay in language development. The first signs may be behavioural changes or problems affecting language. Many have autistic-like features such as poor eye contact, repetitive routines and resistance to change. The pattern of the encephalogram (EEG) is typically abnormal but this may be detected only if special techniques of recording are used. There may be fits but these do not always occur. Steroid drugs give marked improvements in behaviour. Anti-epileptic drugs are also used. A form of brain surgery has been developed to treat this condition and is reported to give good results in some children.

Other neurological conditions

Many physical conditions known to affect the brain can be associated with autistic disorders or aspects of autistic behaviour. Certain conditions that are congenital or that occur in the first year or two of life are particularly likely to be associated with autistic disorders as well as learning difficulties and, often, epilepsy. The major ones are tuberose sclerosis, a genetic condition giving patches of abnormal tissue in the brain, skin and other organs; untreated phenylketonuria, another genetic condition causing a biochemical abnormality that can be treated with a special diet if diagnosed in infancy; some viral and other infections in the mother during pregnancy, particularly rubella; infantile spasms, a rare and severe form of epilepsy occurring in the first year of life. Encephalitis from various kinds of viral infections, especially if it occurs in the early years of life, can also give rise to an autistic disorder. There are various other conditions associated with learning difficulties and epilepsy in which autistic disorders occasionally occur.

A number of other congenital conditions, some known to be genetic while in others the cause is not yet known, often have, in addition to the physical abnormalities, one or more features of behaviour that occur in autistic disorders but not the whole picture. Fragile X has already been mentioned. Two other examples are Williams syndrome, also known as infantile hypercalcaemia, in which repetitive speech and questioning and naive, inappropriate social approaches are common, and Cornelia de Lange syndrome, in which self-injury can be a severe problem. Tourette's syndrome is a neurological disorder in which the symptoms include grunting and twitching, obsessions, uttering of obscenities, attention deficits and overactivity. In any of these conditions, an autistic disorder in its full form can occasionally occur.

Diagnosis of all these conditions depends upon recognition of the physical signs and the history and observation of the behaviour pattern. Autistic behaviour has to be taken into account and properly managed even if it is associated with a known physical condition.

Severe hearing impairments

Children who are born with severe hearing impairments have many problems in learning to understand and use spoken language. They may be difficult in their behaviour and have some features of behaviour seen in autistic children when they are young. However, if they are not autistic as well as hearing-impaired, they form social attachments and are able to use gestures, facial expression, miming and eventually a sign language to communicate and they develop pretend play.

Autistic disorders can occur together with any degree of deafness in which case the dual diagnosis must be made. It is important to make sure that children with autistic behaviour are not also deaf. Testing is often a difficult problem, but the parents' observations of their child's behaviour at home can be most helpful in making a decision.

Severe visual impairments

Some children with severe congenital visual impairments who seem to be developing normally at birth begin to show autistic behaviour in their second or third year of life. Some who are born with a combination of severe visual and hearing impairments have autistic behaviour, especially those affected by maternal rubella. The onset of autistic behaviour in these children, whether from birth or in the second or third year seems likely to be due to associated brain damage rather than the sensory impairments alone.

Some people with congenital visual impairments have stereotyped movements, possibly to compensate for the lack of visual stimulation, but do not have any other features of autistic behaviour.

Developmental language disorders

Children with these difficulties have problems with spoken language. Those with 'receptive' problems have difficulty in understanding words and therefore in learning to speak. Those with 'expressive' problems can understand reasonably well but have difficulty in producing words for themselves. Difficulties with articulation can occur without receptive or expressive disorders. Some children have mixtures of all these aspects of language disorder.

The children with receptive language disorders, especially when young, tend to ignore sounds and to be socially withdrawn. However, if they have the disorder in pure form, they use gestures, eye pointing, facial expression and miming to communicate and can learn a formal sign language. If they learn to read and write they can communicate through writing. They do relate to others and develop imaginative play even if they tend to be immature in behaviour in relation to their physical age. In pure form, receptive language disorders are comparatively rare. Difficulties in language comprehension are, of course, very common in autistic disorders. When children are young, receptive difficulties may be ascribed to a pure language disorder even though other aspects of the triad of impairments are present. This is not helpful for the child or the family since it delays the provision of the right education and advice and help for the parents. The correct diagnosis must be made on a full history and current picture of behaviour, not on language tests alone. There are some children on the borderline between autism and receptive language disorder in whom diagnosis is difficult. The important point is to assess the precise nature of the impairments in each individual child and to tailor the educational and behaviour management programmes to their specific needs.

Children with pure expressive language disorders can understand speech. They can use non-spoken methods of communication, are usually sociable, though immature, and have pretend play. Expressive problems may be associated with poor motor co-ordination. They can also occur together with autistic disorders.

Semantic-pragmatic disorder

The idea of the existence of this syndrome was first put forward only a few years ago. It is described as a condition in which speech production is fluent and grammatically correct but there is a serious deficit in the understanding of speech. There is much repetition and often immediate and delayed echolalia. The children have good memories and may read precociously but with poor understanding. The pragmatic aspect of language is its use in social conversation and its relevance to situations. This is markedly impaired in the syndrome. Some have special interests and repetitive routines. As pointed out by Sarah Lister Brook and Dermot Bowler, who compared the published studies on this subject, this is a description of the 'active but odd' group among the autistic disorders, including those who can be diagnosed as having Asperger's syndrome. Some professional workers who are specialists in linguistics or language therapy insist that the semantic-pragmatic disorder can exist separately from the autistic spectrum. This is usually because they concentrate on language without examining the whole pattern of behaviour and the development from infancy of children given this diagnosis. Most people in the field of autistic disorders do not consider that there is any value in separating semantic-pragmatic disorder from the autistic spectrum. The disadvantage of doing so is the failure to recognize the child's whole pattern of disabilities and therefore a failure to address all their needs. It is also most misleading for the parents.

Disorders of attention, motor co-ordination and perception

Each of these developmental disorders can occur on its own or in combination. They can be associated with language disorders, hyperactivity or underactivity. The perceptual problems include muddling letters in words and letter and word reversals, so are associated with difficulties in learning to read, write and spell. Insistence on following routines and resistance to change are common. Christopher Gillberg and his colleagues in Sweden have found that, among children who have a combination of the disorders of attention, motor coordination and perception, referred to as the DAMP syndrome, there are a number who have diagnosable autistic disorders, especially in the form described by Asperger. As with all developmental disorders, it is important to take a detailed history and to identify each element that may be present and its level of severity, rather than deciding that one of the conditions explains all the other features.

Elective mutism

A small number of children talk in one situation (for example at home) but remain silent elsewhere (for example at school). Shyness and reluctance to speak in strange situations is fairly common in toddlers when first beginning to speak, but if it goes on until school age it is a cause for concern.

'Elective mutism', as this behaviour is called, can be associated with a variety of speech and behaviour problems including autistic disorders. The aim of diagnosis is to find the reason for the behaviour. This, as always, requires a full history from infancy and details of the child's whole pattern of behaviour in different settings, the way language is used when the child does speak and whether the child uses non-spoken methods of communication. The term 'elective mutism' is a name for a specific type of behaviour, not a diagnosis in itself, so does not explain away autistic behaviour if it is present.

Psychiatric conditions

Any type of psychiatric condition can complicate autistic disorders, especially in adolescence and early adult life (see Chapter 14). Difficulties of diagnosis and treatment frequently arise because the psychiatrist, in addition to knowledge of adult psychiatric illness, also has to be aware of autistic spectrum disorders as they appear in adolescents and adults, especially those who are more able. Diagnostic errors are of three types, any of which can lead to inappropriate recommendations for treatment, services and longer-term care.

The first type of error is mistaking an uncomplicated autistic disorder for a psychiatric illness. Adults of borderline, average or high ability with undiagnosed autistic disorders have been wrongly labelled as suffering from any and every psychiatric condition. Among the most common misdiagnoses are obsessive-compulsive disorder, depression and schizophrenia. It is necessary to take a developmental history from a parent covering all the relevant details in order to make the correct diagnosis.

Very rarely, psychiatric conditions usually seen in adolescence or adult life, including schizophrenia, can occur in childhood and lead to strange behaviour. These have to be differentiated from autistic disorders on the history and observation of behaviour. Childhood schizophrenia is extremely rare and has not been reported as beginning before the age of seven. Confusion over diagnosis is most likely with the type of child with an autistic disorder who makes active but odd social approaches and who has a lot of repetitive speech and pseudo-pretend play. The diagnosis of schizophrenia should be made only if the delusions and hallucinations characteristic of that condition are reported by the child, which means that it can be diagnosed only if the child has enough speech.

The diagnosis of 'schizoid personality disorder' has caused some confusion. The term 'personality disorder' is used to cover various patterns of behaviour that are markedly different from the usual culturally accepted range and are consistent and typical of the individual concerned but are not explained by psychiatric illness. The problem is that the factors underlying personality, whether normal or deviant, are still unknown. In the case of 'schizoid personality' the descriptions that have been written of people with this label have certainly included some who had autistic spectrum disorders, especially of the kind described by Asperger. The ICD 10 criteria for schizoid personality disorder include such items as emotional detachment, limited capacity to display warmth to others, consistent choice of solitary activities and no close friends, all of which occur in autistic disorders.

An investigation by Digby Tantam of adults who fitted the diagnostic criteria for 'schizoid personality' showed that many had the developmental history diagnostic of autistic spectrum disorders. Some workers have used the label 'schizoid personality' for young adults who behaved exactly like Asperger described from early childhood onwards. Obviously what has happened is that psychiatrists who work with children and those who work only with adults have each seen the same kinds of people but at different stages of their lives and have given the same people different labels. The range of clinical pictures covered by the term 'schizoid personality disorder' is not identical with autistic spectrum disorders in more able people but there is much overlap. When there is a choice, which label is best? The answer is to choose the one that is most helpful for the person concerned. The label 'personality disorder' is vague and general and has no useful implications. The term 'schizoid personality disorder'

[75]

suggests a link with schizophrenia but there is no evidence that people with autistic conditions are any more likely than anyone else to develop schizophrenia in adult life. Saying that someone has a 'schizoid personality' gives no guidance on treatment or the kinds of help and services they require. In contrast, classification as autistic spectrum disorder, which is recognized as a developmental disorder, leads on to investigation of precisely which aspects of development are affected and then to consideration of what can be done to alleviate the problems. This approach has had major practical implications for ways of helping people with autistic spectrum disorders, so this diagnostic classification is the one to be recommended.

The second type of error is missing a psychiatric illness complicating an autistic disorder. This is easy to do because of the difficulty of obtaining a full and coherent history of symptoms from the person with an autistic disorder. Information from parents or other carers is essential, especially concerning any recent changes from the usual pattern of behaviour.

The third type of error is diagnosing a psychiatric illness but failing to recognize the presence of an underlying autistic disorder. This can happen when there is good evidence of a psychiatric illness but no parent has been asked for a relevant developmental history. It helps if the psychiatrist who diagnoses and treats the psychiatric illness has some experience with adults with autistic disorders and is alert for oddities of social interaction and communication.

Effects of deprivation

Babies and young children who are seriously deprived of stimulating experiences, especially close contact and communication with a caring person, are held back in social, language and intellectual development. They may be so withdrawn and unresponsive that they give the impression of being autistic. Careful observation of the full behaviour pattern shows the differences, but the most important point for diagnosis is the effect of providing the child with better care and wider experiences. The deprived child, within a few weeks or even days of being given such care, begins to make strides in development in all areas. The progress of a child with an autistic disorder, on the other hand, is painfully slow and the basic handicaps remain, even after years of loving care and patient teaching.

Clarke and Clarke, in their book *Early Experience: Myths and Evidence*, give some most interesting examples of deprived children who were eventually rescued and discuss the unsolved question as to how long severe deprivation has to continue before the effects on the child become irreversible. Difficulties in diagnosis arise if a child who has severe learning difficulties or an autistic disorder also happens to be deprived in the early years. The temptation is to explain the handicaps as resulting from the poor environment, but a careful consideration of all the evidence shows the inappropriateness of this type of explanation.

·7·

What causes autistic spectrum disorders?

The history of ideas on the causes of autistic disorders was briefly described in Chapter 1.

When the first edition of this book was written in 1970 there were still many professionals who believed the theories that autism was due to the way parents brought up their children. At that time it was necessary to review in detail the arguments for and against these ideas. There was never any scientific evidence to support this view. As soon as properly controlled studies were carried out it became evident that such theories were wrong. Now, no one with a sound knowledge of research in the field holds such beliefs because the evidence for a physical cause leading to a disorder of development is so strong. The frequency of epilepsy and of generalized learning difficulties is a clinical indicator of brain dysfunction, quite apart from findings from special techniques of examination. The search is on for the nature of the physical cause or, more likely, causes.

Research into causation is being pursued at three different but inter-related levels – these are, the original causes, the site and nature of the pathology in the brain produced by the original causes and the impairments of psychological function produced by the brain pathology, which was produced by the original cause and how these lead to the observable abnormalities of behaviour. It is a scientific version of the House that Jack Built.

Original causes

Studies have shown that a variety of specific medical conditions liable to produce brain pathology can be associated with autistic disorders. Some of these have been mentioned in Chapter 6.

Problems during birth tend to be significantly more common than average among children with autistic disorders. In the past it was thought that these might be the cause of some congenital disabilities, including autism. However, it is now considered that some difficult births are related to pre-existing abnormalities in the child. It appears that the baby has to contribute to the birth process and pre-natal abnormalities in development can cause difficulties. This is of particular interest because there is now a considerable amount of evidence that, in addition to the genetic medical conditions associated with autistic behaviour, such as tuberose sclerosis, genetic factors are important in many cases of autistic disorders. Studies of twins and of family histories have shown positive findings. The patterns in families indicate that the cause is not simply a single dominant or recessive gene. The mechanism must be complex and probably involves more than one gene.

Research teams in different countries are currently engaged in attempts to locate the chromosomes and genes that are responsible for the pathology, particularly in autism of the type described by Kanner, though it is already clear that more than one type of autistic disorder as well as other developmental delays or disabilities can occur within one extended family. A study by Patrick Bolton and his colleagues published in 1994 suggested that, among siblings of children with typical autism, nearly three per cent also had typical autism and the same number had other pervasive developmental disorders (autistic spectrum disorders). The diagnoses were based on the criteria from the international classification system, ICD 10. They also looked for more subtle impairments of communication and social interaction and repetitive patterns of behaviour that were insufficient to justify a diagnosis of an autistic spectrum disorder. They found that 20 per cent had one or more of these impairments in subtle form. The children were compared with a matched group of children with Down's syndrome. They had no siblings with autistic disorders and only three per cent with subtle impairments. It appears that, unless the siblings of children with Down's syndrome are particularly unlikely to have autistic-type impairments, the siblings of children with typical autism are much more likely to have autism or autistic-like traits than the general population.

There are differing opinions among research workers as to the proportion of children whose typical autism appears to be due to an identifiable medical condition. The best estimates come from epidemiological studies where all eligible children are seen and examined because, if a child has, for instance, tuberose sclerosis, associated autism may not be recognized and no referral made to a specialist clinic. Figures from the epidemiological studies of typical autism vary because of differences in selection criteria but it appears that about one quarter have an identifiable medical condition likely to have caused the autism. Such conditions are most likely to be found among those with severe or profound generalized learning difficulties though they can occur in individuals of any level of ability.

No detailed studies of medical conditions associated with the Asperger picture have as yet been carried out but individual cases with, for example, tuberose sclerosis, have been reported. It is known that problems during birth are common in people with the behaviour described by Asperger.

The pathology in the brain

How and where do the original causes affect the brain? Do all types of causes home in on the same brain structures and functions or are there different pathological pictures that can all give rise to autistic behaviour? Do different sub-groups have different types of brain dysfunctions? These questions remain to be answered but advances in brain imaging techniques, neuroanatomy, physiology and biochemistry have all contributed to the research on normal brain function and on brain pathology.

Over the years, various theories as to the brain areas affected have been put forward. The latest research suggests that the parts of the brain called the limbic system and the cerebellum are involved. A post mortem study of six brains from individuals who had autism of the kind described by Kanner, by Margaret Bauman and Thomas Kemper in the USA, in their book *The Neurobiology of Autism*, showed abnormalities in these areas at the microscopic level that probably dated from before birth. Pre-natal lesions in these areas are likely to interfere with processing of all kinds of information coming in through the senses and to have marked effects on learning, emotional responses and behaviour in general. The findings can be linked with the fact that rote memory in autism is often good, while memory requiring items of information to be associated and processed is poor.

Research is also continuing on the neurochemicals that are involved in transmission of messages in the brain and on physiological measures of brain activity. Results so far have been inconsistent but improvement in techniques, including new ways of brain imaging, will, it is hoped, produce more conclusive findings in the future. There is now interest in hormones, such as oxytocin, that affect early brain development.

Psychological dysfunctions

All kinds of studies of different aspects of psychological dysfunctions have been carried out in the attempt to identify the nature of the impairment, or impairments, that underlie the characteristic behaviour, especially the triad of impairments. These include investigations of language, memory, attention and visuo-spatial skills. The most recent development in this area arose out of work on the growth in normal children of understanding of other people's thoughts and feelings. This developmental skill is referred to as the 'Theory of Mind'. Uta Frith and Simon Baron-Cohen and their colleagues investigated this in children with autism of the kind described by Kanner and found marked impairments. This fits well with the typical social indifference in young children with autism and the social naivety of the older, more able individuals.

[81]

With further investigation, complications became evident – a familiar experience in research. The level of development of theory of mind, even in autism, is related to language comprehension. Some children can pass the simpler tests, though are defeated by more complex theory of mind tasks. When young adults with the pattern described by Asperger are tested, some are able to pass all the tests although they show a marked lack of understanding of other people in real-life situations. As Uta Frith has pointed out, the tests of theory of mind that have been devised to date are designed for research and should *not* be used for diagnosis of autistic conditions. Passing these tests does not rule out the diagnosis. More sophisticated tests need to be developed to reveal the precise nature of the social impairment.

As discussed in Chapter 2, it seems that people with autistic disorders have great difficulty in seeing, or rather feeling, meaning in their experiences. Instead of developing the usual pattern of priorities that are common to humanity, though modified by culture, only a few things have emotional significance for people with autistic disorders and these tend to be idiosyncratic to the person concerned and usually of little use in adapting to life. The research into how the brain assigns significance to objects and events may prove to be of great relevance to autistic disorders.

Four problems have to be considered in relation to all research in this field. First, because autistic disorders can be associated with various conditions affecting the brain, the abnormalities that are specific to autism have to be distinguished from others that may be present. Second, the problems related to autism have to be separated from those due to any associated learning difficulties. This is difficult because learning difficulties can occur as a consequence of autistic disorders as well as from other conditions that may be present and that may or may not be linked with the autism. Third, the features, such as odd responses to sensory stimuli and motor problems, that are very common in autistic disorders but are not considered essential for diagnosis, also have to be accounted for in any comprehensive theory of causation. Fourth, the difficulties of definition of autistic disorders make it hard to compare studies. Interview and observation schedules have been designed to obtain detailed clinical information to aid in ensuring comparability between samples of subjects used for research. These are helpful but do not entirely solve the problems.

Much of the research to date has concentrated on children who have autism of the Kanner type. More recently, those with the behaviour described by Asperger have been investigated. It would be interesting and helpful to extend research to cover all those with the triad of impairments and to include adults of all ages as well as children. Another approach to research in the field would be to compare the pathology in autistic disorders with that in conditions, such as Fragile X, in which some but not all aspects of the autistic picture are found.

Part 2

WAYS OF HELPING

·8·

Making sense of time and space

Autistic disorders affect all the activities of daily living and they are usually lifelong, though tending to slow improvement. There is no known cure for these disabilities, but this does not mean that nothing can be done. Those affected can be helped to compensate for their difficulties with special methods of education, both at home and at school. In many ways the problem is similar to that faced by the parents and teachers of children with hearing or visual impairments that cannot be cured. The children can be helped through education to develop to their full potential, however large or small this may be, and the adults can be given the opportunities to make the best use of the skills they do possess. Some of the children have too many additional disabilities to make much progress but, even in these cases, it is worth trying to encourage more appropriate behaviour and to teach simple self-care. For those who are more able much more can be achieved.

In many ways, the learning difficulties and inappropriate behaviour found in autistic spectrum disorders are similar to those found in other developmental disabilities and many of the general principles underlying methods of teaching and caring can be applied. However, the basic autistic inability to make sense of past and present experiences leads to special difficulties in comprehending time and space. Programmes for teaching or caring are successful only if these difficulties are understood and taken into account. In the rest of this book, many more examples of problems in time and space and suggestions for ways of helping will be given under different headings but this aspect of the autistic disorders is so important for understanding how the children and adults see the world that it needs a whole chapter to itself.

The problems with time are not related to telling time by the clock, which some people with autistic disorders are able to do well. The difficulties lie in comprehending the passage of time and linking it with ongoing activities. This often shows itself as an inability to wait. Impatience is common in all young children but in people with autistic disorders it can continue for years, even into adult life. Some begin to scream if made to wait more than a second for their food, for a walk, for a ride in the car or for anything else that they want. Another aspect of poor understanding of time is seen when trying to persuade a child to wash, dress and generally prepare for school or some other event within the time available. Even the most able individuals may find it impossible to cope with time limits and this can be a major barrier to becoming independent.

One of the most obvious examples of confusion with time is the way in which those with enough speech continually ask for reassurance about future events and when they will happen. They want to have the timetable spelt out in precise detail, not once but an infinite number of times. Parents and teachers are tempted to ascribe this to a desire for attention or to be annoying but the underlying anxiety associated with the questions shows that there is a real difficulty in understanding that the future will eventually become the present. Another aspect of this problem is the lack of awareness that an event, once started, will come to an end. Some children have been extremely distressed when taken on some new expedition because they did not know if they would ever return home again and did not have the words to ask. The fear generated by being lost in time also explains why there is often such a strong adverse reaction to any unpredicted change in the expected timetable. Some more able children who can tell time by the clock become obsessed with time and demand that everything happens at the precise pre-ordained moment. Woe betide the parent of such a child who promises to do something in 'just five minutes' and then takes six minutes and 14 seconds.

The trouble with time is that it cannot be seen or felt but has to be inferred from the sequence of events. There is some similarity with speech, which has no visible, tangible form and has gone as soon as the words have been uttered. It seems that people with autistic disorders have severe problems with coping with sequential events that have no independent, concrete existence. Concepts of time have always puzzled and fascinated philosophers but most people are born with the ability to understand it in everyday terms. People with autistic disorders seem to lack this understanding to a degree that is markedly discrepant with their level of intelligence.

The best way to help is to represent the passage of time in practical terms – the abstract has to be made concrete. Visual timetables are invaluable. They can be composed of drawings, photographs, words if the child can read, or a combination of these. The days can be divided into segments marked by meal and snack times. The sequence of time can shown by the progression of days from left to right, in countries where this is the convention for writing. Each child should have their own timetable. The day can begin with the child going through the pictured events of that day with the help of a parent or teacher. Some children like to mark the previous day to show that it has gone. When talking through the timetable, the end of each event should be explained as well as its beginning – 'After lunch we shall go to the park and play on the swings. Then we shall come back home again'. When setting out on any expedition, it should be made clear that it will end in a return to home or other base.

Such timetables are useful for introducing planned changes into the programme. Unplanned changes should be avoided if at all possible. If they do happen at short notice, as much explanation and reassurance as possible should be given. Some children like to have any unexpected changes inserted into their personal timetable as a record of the past that they can talk about afterwards. The timetables should be kept so that they can be used to talk about the past as well as the future. This can be a source of much pleasure for some children. Parents often say how sad it is that their children do not seem to recall happy events, or to look forward to enjoyable occasions, especially Christmas or other special festivals, because this means they lack two of the major sources of pleasure in life. Making and keeping records of past and future events helps to develop appreciation of past pleasures and those to come. Photographs, slides and videos can all be used for this purpose.

The passing of shorter periods of time can also be marked by cues. A child can be helped to stay on task or to wait quietly for something to happen if the end of the time allotted or the waiting period is marked in some way. Unless the child can tell the time by the clock it is not usually possible for them to comprehend that time is moving by looking at either a digital or an analogue clock. It is easier for them if the end of a time period is marked with an alarm or kitchen timer. Alternatively, time can be made visible by using a device like the computer method of showing the progress of a program by gradually colouring in a long rectangle.

More able children also need assistance in organizing themselves. The problems are particularly acute in mainstream school. Personal timetables, written lists of, for example, the things they have to take to school each day, written instructions and maps to show them when and where to go if they have lessons in more than one classroom, can ease their way through school. Someone to whom they can always turn for help and who understands the reasons for their confusion is essential. The same kind of help is needed for adults in open employment.

People with autistic disorders also have problems in understanding boundaries and relationships between objects in space. Among the very young and those who are very severely disabled, there may be confusion about the parts of their own bodies. For example, at the age of five years a girl with autism was still regarding her own hand emerging from a sleeve as if she had never seen it before. The children may find it hard to relate images of the same object seen from different points of view, which may explain why they often closely examine objects from different angles. They may be unaware of the boundaries between objects that to others seem so obvious. For example, they may not know where their own house ends and the next one begins. They are usually quite unaware of the subtle boundaries that are not physically marked, such as other people's personal space, or the areas on the crowded beach occupied by other families. It is not surprising that they are baffled by the complex relationships between people.

To help reduce the confusion, boundaries in space and time and relationships between people, objects and events have to be explained in as simple a way as possible using every available way of expressing concepts in visual terms. An album of photographs of familiar places can be used as a teaching aid. Looking through the pictures every day, naming things in them and retelling stories of events involving the child is an activity that many of the children enjoy. It is a useful substitute for a bedtime story for those who are not interested in fiction.

People with autistic disorders lack an internal structure for their lives. They need to have an external framework constructed for them by those who care for them and teach them. Even those who are most able need this type of support. The most successful find it for themselves in the work and living arrangements they choose but even they are vulnerable if the structure is completely removed by the hazards of life.

Whatever you do in this life, there is always a down side. In this case the disadvantage is that, when a child with an autistic disorder appreciates and is helped by a timetable, it can become a repetitive routine that must not be changed under any circumstances. Using the technique to introduce changes deliberately helps to overcome this. On balance, despite possible problems, the positive gains of using timetables outweigh the negative.

The triad of impairments

The cluster of impairments of social interaction, communication and imagination and the consequent repetitive pattern of behaviour is the common thread connecting all autistic disorders, whatever other conditions may be present. Teachers with training and experience in the field are developing methods of helping children to compensate for these disabilities and a range of books and papers is available. Here, the aim is to give some simple ideas that parents can use in everyday situations.

Social interaction

This is the aspect of autistic conditions that causes parents the most heartache and feelings of inadequacy and guilt that are totally undeserved.

DEVELOPING SOCIAL CONTACT

The young child with typical autism of the kind described by Kanner appears aloof and indifferent to others and happy in his or her own world unless someone interferes. One of the barriers to making contact with such a child can be dislike of being touched. This can make washing and dressing a nightmare and cause the child to resist being held by the hand when out walking. Paradoxically, the children usually enjoy rough-and-tumble play and this can be used to give them the feeling that contact with other people can be enjoyable. The play sessions can begin with more active play and then gradually become quieter and more gentle. This type of contact can be associated with other experiences that are enjoyed, such as a mid-morning drink or biscuit. If the child likes music, as so many of them do, they may be happy to sit on a parent's lap and be rocked while listening to a favourite tune. They may be more receptive to this after some physical activity or after a bath. It may be necessary to start with a few seconds of contact only and then gradually to increase the time.

Some aspects of appropriate social behaviour can be taught, even though they are used in a mechanical way. Eye contact does tend to improve with increasing age but it can be encouraged. Providing this does not cause distress, the child's head can be gently held to attract their visual attention when talking to them. Some will make eye contact if the adult pulls funny faces, or sings a favourite song. One game that a little girl enjoyed was touching noses with her mother who then twisted her head to create a funny visual effect. The child happily made eye contact to ask for this game and then used it for other requests.

Positive signs of affection within the family can also be taught. Instead of allowing the child to accept a hug and a kiss passively, their own arms can be guided to return the hug. It is best for the child to learn this as a response to affection from others rather than encouraging them to initiate the contact, in case they assume that this is the way to greet everyone.

A child can be taught to shake hands if their hand is guided correctly whenever a visitor offers a hand first. Again, it is better to teach this as a response to a proffered hand rather than encouraging the child to make the first move, since they will not understand when it is correct to do this and when not. With the children who can speak, teaching polite behaviour, such as saying please and thank you, is worthwhile. They have no idea why people do this but it helps to make them more socially acceptable.

Although they lack the inbuilt social instinct, the children do, in the course of time, become attached in their own way to the people who care for them. This is partly due to the fact that their parents or other carers become familiar to them and partly because they provide the things the child wants. This is 'cupboard love' to start with but it does grow into something deeper over the years. It is never the same as instinctive feelings but it is no less genuine. The attachment grows most easily if parents are calm and consistent in their approach, provide a clear framework of rules that apply to all the family and give the child some pleasant experiences to make up for the fact that ordinary life tends to be a constant source of anxiety and confusion for them.

Sisters and brothers, especially if they are of an age at which they are willing and eager to play, also become important to a child with an autistic disorder. Often, the sibling leads the child with an autistic disorder into all kinds of activities in which they would not otherwise engage. The fact that the child is mostly or always a passive partner does not matter. The experience of play is of benefit.

Even if they relate well to siblings, it is easier for the children to relate to adults than to children outside the family, especially those of the same age. This is probably because adults are able to adapt themselves to the child, whereas other children, unless they also have siblings who are autistic, do not have the necessary insight and do not modify their behaviour. Most children with autistic disorders with moderate or severe handicaps will always need adult supervision and guidance whenever they are with a group of same age children. They must be protected from bullying and teasing. Children with autistic disorders cannot defend themselves and do not learn to do so through experience. They have neither the verbal wit nor the physical skills to hold their own among their peers. The situation must never be allowed to degenerate so that the autistic child reacts with random aggression, or else withdraws and wanders away on his own.

So far I have concentrated upon ways of encouraging social mixing. The other side of the picture can be seen in some children who make good progress. They may become over-friendly and sociable in an immature way and fail to discriminate between people they know and complete strangers. One girl of 10 would rush up to strangers with a joyful greeting, to their amazement. Her parents had to restrain her and explain many times over that she must not talk to people in the street unless her parents made the first move. She was most upset at first, but the phase passed after a few months. There is no easy answer, since parents do not want to discourage a spontaneous friendliness that they have spent so long in encouraging. However, I have not met any children who have become withdrawn again because their over-friendliness has had to be curbed.

EXPEDITIONS, HOLIDAYS AND SOCIAL OCCASIONS

Trips out with parents, brothers and sisters are a part of family social life. Young children with autistic disorders often find crowds and bustle confusing and frightening. At this stage, family expeditions should be carefully planned. They should be kept fairly short and not too far from home, so that it is easy to remove the child if the situation proves too distressing. Different kinds of outings can be tried. If one is not a success, then it is best to leave it for a while and try again later. A visit to the zoo, with lively, noisy, smelly animals, may terrify a young child but be enjoyed when the child is older. When the child is able to understand, they can be prepared in advance by explaining in words and pictures where they are going, what will happen there, how long it will last and, very important, that they will, in the end, return home. Details, such as when and where they will eat and whether there are toilets and, if not, how they will cope, have to be included in the story.

Most young children with autistic disorders do not understand the point of birthday parties and do not participate if parents invite other children and there is no point in trying to make them take part. Older and more able children may like to go to parties although they may join in very little. One boy who liked sitting and watching the other children at parties was sad when his sisters were invited without him. The hosts had not realized that, in his own quiet way, he was enjoying himself. Parents, who so often have to stand between the world and their child, need to overcome any diffidence they feel and explain to friends and relations, so that the child has as much social life as possible. When the family entertains, the child with an autistic disorder may enjoy having a special role, such as handing round dishes of nuts or sweets, or clearing the table after the meal. This has to be practised in advance and the guests primed to express praise and appreciation, if this pleases the child.

Although some children with autistic disorders are afraid of trains or buses, many love travelling in any form of transport and may be calmer and happier when on the move than in any other situation. However, apart from the actual journey, holidays away from home may be difficult. A young child may be bewildered by new surroundings and may never settle during the whole period away from home. Many families do not take a vacation, or else try to arrange temporary residential care for the child while the rest of the family goes away. The problems often lessen as the child grows older. A short break should be tried first. A self-catering holiday away from other people has obvious advantages.

As always, advance preparation of the child using pictures to explain exactly what will happen makes all the difference to the children who can understand. Some of the child's favourite possessions should be taken and the activities planned so that the child is kept amused and happy as much as possible. The aim is to associate going away on holiday with happy occasions so that eventually trips become easier to organize. The effort is worthwhile because new experiences that the child enjoys help to build confidence in place of fear. One child found it difficult to tolerate a long journey to a holiday destination the first time this was tried. She had no idea how long the journey would take and what would happen at the end, despite the parents' attempts to explain. She was able to recognize and match written words so, on the next long journey, she was given a list of all the towns and villages on the route. The signs with the names on were pointed out and she crossed them off her list as they were passed. This proved an enjoyable occupation and showed her, in visual terms, the length of the journey.

Communication

In the first edition of this book, I included a description of a method intended to teach children with autistic disorders to speak, used by psychologists who advocated the 'operant conditioning' approach. Briefly, the technique was gradually to 'shape' the sounds made by the child by rewarding nearer and nearer approximations to words. Even then, there was considerable doubt as to the effectiveness of this system. Now it is clear that the language impairments in autistic disorders are primarily due to the lack of the normally innate drive to communicate with others. There may or may not be developmental language disorders in addition to this fundamental impairment but the communication problems cannot be overcome simply by teaching the children to speak, even if that were possible.

Within the whole autistic spectrum, including those who are most able, the majority of children do develop speech sooner or later and most do so without any specialist help. The problem is that this speech is based on a vocabulary that is learnt by rote, although those who make the most progress do become very fluent with a large store of words. The best way for parents to try to encourage the communicative use of speech is to give the child as wide a range as possible of social and other experiences. Preparing in advance with words and pictures and retelling events afterwards with more words and pictures provide the opportunity for the child to make connections between events and to learn that words have meanings in the real world. If a video camera is available, video-tapes of special occasions are useful for gaining the attention of some children. Even if videos can be made, still photographs have their advantages as well because they capture one single moment in time. The ordinary events of everyday life as well as special trips and treats provide plenty of material for these sessions. This type of interaction with parents and siblings helps the children to develop some awareness that talking to others can be interesting and rewarding.

The abnormalities of speech that are characteristic of autistic disorders were described in Chapter 4. It is not helpful to correct these odd ways of speaking. It is more important to encourage the child to communicate in whatever way they can. Where appropriate, rephrasing the child's utterances when replying, without criticizing, is more useful.

In contrast to the children who speak very little, there are some who talk repetitively and far too much. Their speech is not used for two-way communication. The same ideas for enlarging experiences and using them to develop understanding are just as relevant for these children.

For children with no or very limited speech, the signs the child does use, such as indicating by touching or pointing, should be encouraged. If a child has no other means of expressing their needs, it is preferable for them to lead someone by the arm to show what is wanted than to scream. At this stage, the parent can teach the child, by repetition, to respond to the words 'Show me' while putting out a hand to be taken. Every opportunity should be taken to reward more appropriate methods of communicating but any method is better than nothing. Teaching a manual sign language, such as the Makaton system, can be tried although, almost always, the same limitations and abnormalities are found in signed as in spoken speech. Just occasionally a child learns to use signs much better than speech. Presumably this occurs when the child has an additional developmental disorder affecting expressive speech but has sufficient inner language to allow them to express more in signs. For this reason, it is always worth trying to teach a sign language but the child should not be pressurized to use it if there is little or no progress.

Imagination

Pretend play is the earliest indicator of the development of imagination. Like speech, it is either conspicuous by its absence or repetitive if present. Some children will learn a sequence of actions, such as preparing, pouring out and offering a pretend cup of tea, but true creativity in play, especially that shared with other children, cannot be taught. Sometimes sisters or brothers involve the children in pretend games, assigning them a role they can carry out as directed.

The children who have repetitive 'pretend' play, including acting out scenes from videos or other sources, do have a way of occupying themselves, which can be a relief for parents. If the child becomes so involved in one activity that it takes over from all other activities, then limiting the time spent on such play is necessary. This does involve parents in the task of finding other activities to replace the repetitive play.

The value of true imagination and creativity is in associating past and present experiences and making plans for the future, ranging from the mundane what to do tomorrow to the grand plans for the whole of life. The impairment of this aspect of development in people with autistic disorders is a constantly repeated theme throughout this book because it has such wide and deep implications for their lives. Ways of helping the children to conceptualize past, present and future by representing them in visual terms have been described in Chapter 8.

Resistance to change and repetitive activities

This type of behaviour ranks high on the list of problems that cause parents the most worry and despair. If not handled properly, a child's insistence on routine can come to dominate the life of the whole family.

The behaviour is the child's attempt to introduce order into their chaotic world and this has to be remembered when working out the best way of managing the problem. It is necessary to arrange the child's life so that it has order and pattern. Some kind of repetitive behaviour is inevitably present in a child with an autistic disorder and this has to be accepted. A firm line needs to be drawn when the routine or resistance to change reaches the point where it interferes with the life of the rest of the family and prevents the child from moving forward to more constructive activities.

The solution depends upon the nature of the routine. If the child insists on holding an object in their hand that is large and attracts adverse attention in public, or prevents other activities in which the hand would be used, or leads to other difficulties, the system of gradual reduction may be successful. One small girl insisted on holding a piece of photographic negative in her hand. Whenever the negative became creased or torn, which inevitably happened sooner or later, she screamed loud and long until a new piece was provided. Her parents decided to make the negatives a tiny bit smaller each day. She did not bother about this gradual change. Eventually the stage was reached when the piece of negative was about one centimetre square. At this point a new problem emerged. The little girl held this in the centre of the palm of her right hand with the tip of her middle finger. As soon as it became damp with perspiration, which occurred very frequently, she had a temper tantrum, though she did not release her grip on the fragment of negative. Eventually, her parents decided not to give her any more pieces and to ignore the screams. After a difficult day or two, the child lost the last fragment and the routine disappeared.

Some objects cannot be cut down in size. One strategy that can be used is to allow the child to have the object at certain times and not at others. If, for any reason, the times when the object is to be allowed has to be reduced, this should be done gradually. Much determination is needed to start the process of time restriction but, once established, it becomes part of the child's routine. One girl, at 10 years of age, wanted to carry a large dustpan and brush with her all the time. Her parents insisted that she left it at home whenever she left the house. After a few protests she accepted the new routine of putting the dustpan and brush in one particular place and saying, 'All ready for come back' when she went out.

There are other kinds of collecting that cannot be tackled by these methods. The case of the boy who wanted to hold empty detergent packets has already been mentioned in a previous chapter. He could find the packets in any house he was taken to visit and would run into a stranger's house if the door was open. If he found a packet with powder in, he would empty it in the sink or on the floor. The only way his parents could deal with this was to prevent it altogether. They hid their own detergent packets, visited only friends and relations who understood and would do the same and kept a tight hold on the child's hand when out walking. They did not take him into any shop that sold detergents. After a few weeks, he had lost interest in this pursuit. If it is decided that some behaviour of this kind has to be stopped and it cannot be done gradually, the policy of total prevention is the most likely to succeed, if it is possible to put this into effect.

Some children involve other people in their routines. One child insisted that everyone in the family sat on the same chair at each meal. His temper tantrums if the pattern was disturbed made it impossible for the family to have guests for a meal. To overcome the problem, the rest of the family decided to change their places at every meal, regardless of the tantrums. The child's protests became louder and longer for several days, then diminished over a few days and finally stopped completely.

Bedtime routines present particular problems. The children who have them may not settle to sleep until a complex sequence of actions involving the parents has been completed without error. It may be possible to diminish the routines by missing out a tiny step every few nights. Refusal to allow the routine at all is likely to lead to tantrums and refusal to settle to sleep for some time. It is not possible to predict how long the protest might last. If the routine is not too taxing to carry out it is easiest to accept it, especially if the child then sleeps peacefully. It is worth taking a stand only if it is very long and complicated or if it seems to be growing in length and complexity.

Often, parents who have had the courage to tackle a particular routine have found that, once the problem has been overcome, the child seems more aware of them in a positive way. The parents gain confidence in their ability to help their child and the child finds that giving up a routine does not make the world fall to pieces. He or she has been helped to take a small step forward and all the family gain from the experience.

It is one of the basic facts of autistic disorders that, if one routine disappears, another comes along to take its place. However, if one is overcome successfully by the parents, those that follow tend to present less of a problem. In theory it should be possible to deal with each routine as it occurs. In practice, most parents find that a compromise works well. Some of the habits comfort the child but do not cause any problems and these can be left alone. For example, it does not matter if a child likes to carry a particular small object in a pocket, as long there is no tantrum if it is lost. Effort should be saved for tackling routines that do have adverse effects on the child or the family.

Once parents have made up their minds to discourage the unacceptable routines, it is helpful to deal with a new one that might be troublesome as soon as it appears. The task is easier in the early stages than it is once the routine is well established. A number of mothers take deliberate steps to vary household practices just a little every day so that the children become used to the idea of a certain amount of change. This may seem to contradict the rule that autistic children need order in their lives. The aim is to find a balance between too much rigidity on the one hand and too little structure on the other. How this is worked out depends on the individual child and the family concerned.

·10·

Reducing inappropriate behaviour

When a child with an autistic disorder begins to walk, the pattern of autistic behaviour usually becomes obvious, whether or not there were signs during the first year or so. Parents have to begin the long process of helping their child to adapt to the family and the world. The problems they meet during the years of childhood are many and varied and each child has his own special difficulties as well as those that are common to most of the children. All I can do here is to write about some of the situations with which parents have to cope and to make some suggestions based on ideas that have proven helpful in practice.

It is easiest to consider ways of helping under two main headings. In this chapter I shall suggest ways of reducing inappropriate behaviour. The following chapter will deal with methods for encouraging the development of skills. For each of these topics, I shall give some general rules, followed by practical examples of ways of helping the children.

These two chapters are concerned with children, including those with autistic disorders and learning difficulties in severe form. The special problems and needs of adolescents and adults and of those who are more able will be considered in later chapters. However, the ideas in the discussion that follows are basic to all autistic disorders and have relevance at all ages and for all levels of ability.

General principles

It is now the fashion to refer to difficult behaviour as 'challenging'. This term was chosen with the best of political intentions but the result has not always been that desired by those coining the phrase. It was meant to suggest that the behaviour 'challenged' the carers to find ways of helping the person concerned. Instead, it is often thought of by those not in the field as behaviour that is deliberately awkward and defiant, which excludes many of the types of behaviour problems common in autistic disorders. The term 'inappropriate' behaviour seems to me to be both neutral and descriptive.

Until they know the reason, having a child with unusual and socially inappropriate behaviour makes most parents feel that it is their fault, even though the other children in the family may behave impeccably. These feelings are unjustified because the ordinary methods of bringing up children, based largely on the supposition that the child understands what you say, has some desire to please and a growing awareness of the consequences of their actions, do not work with children with autistic disorders.

In the first edition of this book, I discussed methods of rigid 'behaviour management' developed by psychologists and used with children with autistic disorders among others. These were based on theories of how people learn patterns of behaviour through reward and punishment. At that time, there was much interest in these ideas and hope that the methods would produce major improvements in behaviour and level of ability. Over the years since then, the limitations, especially in regard to children with autistic disorders, have become apparent. Behaviour management techniques do not help the children to learn more than their in-built potential allows. The methods may sometimes, but by no means always, help to control behaviour while they are being applied but, as soon as they cease, the previous behaviour returns. It was found that people with autistic disorders do not generalize any improvement in behaviour or skills seen in one setting to other situations. Behaviour management methods do not change the individual with an autistic disorder in any fundamental way – useful results, if any, are temporary.

Apart from the lack of permanent effects in autistic disorders, there have been two other major criticisms. First, in the early years, some psychologists used harsh methods of discouraging inappropriate behaviour that would now be considered to be abuse. In any case, many children with autistic disorders appear indifferent to physical punishment, have no notion of shame and tend to regard a punishment as an automatic part of a repetitive routine that is sought for rather than experienced as a deterrent. Second, the pioneers thought that the reasons for any behaviour were irrelevant to its management and all one had to do was to apply the method strictly according to the rules. It is difficult to understand how anyone could hold this view.

Although experience has shown the limitations of psychological methods of managing behaviour, there are some general principles that parents and professionals have found useful, even if they do not solve all the problems. The first task is to sort out, if possible, the reasons for the inappropriate behaviour. Here is a list of the most frequent.

1 Interference with the usual daily routine or with the individual's own repetitive activities is perhaps the most frequent cause of difficult, inappropriate behaviour. Alterations in tiny, trivial details may be enough to start a major temper tantrum.

2 Confusion and fear produced by unfamiliar events and situations.

3 Inability to understand explanations, reassurance or instructions.

4 Lack of knowledge of the social rules for behaviour.

5 Inability to communicate needs and feelings in words or signs.

6 Oversensitivity to noise, bright lights, being touched, too close proximity of other people. Even smells can be the cause of intense distress and inappropriate behaviour.

7 Specific fears (phobias) of harmless objects or situations.

8 Pressure to do tasks that are too difficult or that are disliked or go on too long.

9 Although other reasons are more common, parents and carers should consider the possibility that inappropriate behaviour is due to discomfort, pain or illness, especially if it is different in form or timing from the usual pattern.

Some general rules for coping with inappropriate behaviour can also be listed although the way they are applied depends on the reasons for the behaviour. The first seven of these are especially relevant for people with autistic disorders.

1 The first and most important rule has been emphasized. The environment and the daily routine must be structured, organized and predictable. The lack of ability to process information means that the person with an autistic disorder lives in a confusing and frighteningly unpredictable world. An organized environment and routine are vital in order to give them a feeling of order and stability.

2 Changes to the routine need to be planned and, if possible, introduced slowly. Ways have to be found to let the child or adult know in advance, as accurately as possible, what will happen. This is particularly important if there is to be a temporary or permanent change of carer for any reason. Attempts to change the child's own repetitive routines work best if carried out gradually, if this is possible.

3 Methods of communication have to be adapted to ensure that the child or adult understands what is wanted.

4 Ways need to be found to cope with aspects of the environment that cause distress, such as the level of noise, too bright lighting or the presence of something that is frightening for the child concerned.

5 Pressure to perform above the individual's level of ability must be avoided.

6 General health care and watchfulness for signs of injury or illness as shown by the individual child are important.

7 There is evidence that regular physical exercise tends to diminish aggressive behaviour and stereotypies in people with autistic disorders as well as having beneficial effects on health.

The last six rules come from general theories about learning.

8 Behaviour that is rewarded is more likely to be repeated, while behaviour that is not rewarded is less likely to be repeated. With people with autistic disorders, the difficulty is knowing what counts as a reward. It can be something that others find uninteresting or even thoroughly unpleasant. Even the simple fact that an action has been carried out in a certain way is enough to begin a cycle of exact repetition.

9 With inappropriate behaviour, the best strategy is to prevent it occurring at all because it is so easy for people with autistic disorders to get into a repetitive cycle once they have started doing some action or sequence of actions.

10 If an inappropriate behaviour cannot be prevented, it should not be rewarded.

11 If at all possible, a different and more constructive activity should be provided and rewarded to replace the inappropriate behaviour. The reward has to be relevant for the child concerned.

12 Timing is crucial. The response to behaviour, whether it is to be encouraged or discouraged, should be timed so that it is quite clear that it is the behaviour that produces the response. The poorer the understanding of language, the more important this is.

13 Inconsistency of response to inappropriate behaviour, for example, sometimes ignoring, sometimes scolding and sometimes giving an ice cream to stop a temper tantrum tends to make the behaviour worse and certainly does not make it better.

These rules are not easy to follow in a family home, especially if there are other children, but they are worth attempting. Patience and perseverance are needed because results may not be seen for weeks, months or years. It helps a great deal to remain calm and avoid negative emotional reactions whatever the provocation. It cannot be said too often that the outward signs of anger are no help at all because many children and adults with autistic disorders find them interesting and rewarding and try to induce them again. It is helpful if parents work together and are consistent in the way they respond to inappropriate behaviour.

The following are some examples of the way the rules can be applied in practice, in response to particular aspects of behaviour in autistic disorders.

Temper tantrums and aggression

Tantrums, which may be accompanied by biting, scratching or other aggressive acts towards self or others, are common in children with autistic disorders. Methods of coping work best, and are in the best interests of the child and the whole family, if they take into account the reasons for the tantrums, though these may be difficult to discover. It is helpful to observe the situations in which tantrums occur to see if there is any pattern. Keeping notes is well worthwhile even if difficult to maintain consistently in the family situation. When causes or precipitating factors are known, these should be eliminated or avoided if at all possible. If they cannot be avoided, at least the knowledge allows parents to anticipate and be ready to cope with the adverse reactions. When a tantrum or an aggressive act occurs, parents should respond in a calm, low-key way and should defuse the situation as soon as possible by, if necessary, removing the child from the place where the problem occurred and involving them in another activity. If a child tends to attack a sibling when upset, this should be anticipated and prevented. Cooperation between all those caring for a child, planning in advance how to manage difficult behaviour and consistency in response are particularly important in reducing physical aggression towards others.

The problems of tantrums in response to interference with repetitive routines have already been mentioned and ways of coping discussed.

Young children with autistic disorders often have tantrums simply because they want to be given something, such as a biscuit or drink. Parents, understandably, tend to deal with the situation by giving the child what they want to soothe and quieten them because they know from bitter experience that the screams can go on for hours. Unfortunately, this is a good way to demonstrate the truth of one of the basic rules of learning theory – behaviour that is rewarded tends to increase in frequency. In other words, the child finds out through practical experience that the quickest way to get anything they want is to scream, shout, stamp, kick, bite – in short to have a first-class temper tantrum. This behaviour is one of the very limited options for a child with no useful spoken or signed language.

There are two aspects to changing this type of behaviour. The first is to make sure that the children are never given the things they want while actually having a tantrum. This requires strong nerves and determination because the policy must be put into practice in public, as well as at home. If a child has a tantrum because they have seen something they want in the street or in a shop, the only solution may be to remove them from the scene as rapidly but with as little fuss and as calmly as possible. In the home, some form of distraction may work, or holding the child while rocking and singing to them, if they like this, until the tantrum ceases, or ignoring the tantrum altogether. Experience shows what works best. If what the child wants is reasonable, it can be given when the tantrum stops but not before.

The second way of reducing temper tantrums used as demands is to encourage the development of more appropriate forms of communication, as discussed in Chapter 9. Even in children who have adequate understanding of speech or signs, tantrums may occur if requests are refused. Many of them react very badly to the word 'No'. This is true of any young child but it is particularly evident in those with autistic disorders. It is a good idea to avoid the direct use of this word and of the sharp, negative tone of voice that goes with it. It is possible to use other, calmly spoken words for refusing or, if appropriate, deferring requests.

Screaming may be due to fear and distress produced by something that is in reality quite harmless. If this goes on for long, the child may lose all control and behave in exactly the same way as in a temper tantrum. When the cause is known, the child can be removed from the fear-provoking situation and comforted. Holding, cuddling and talking or singing in a soothing way until the child calms down is particularly appropriate for helping to reduce fear. The causes of the fear must be dealt with and some suggestions for this will be given below.

Some of the children resist and have tantrums in response to care procedures, especially hair washing, brushing, combing or cutting. The problem may be sensitivity to being touched, resistance to any interference, or it may be due to real fear. If the child dislikes being touched, it is important to be as gentle and reassuring as possible. If it is simply dislike of the interference, making the procedure part of the regular routine and calm, quiet persistence usually help the child to accept eventually. Distraction, such as playing a piece of music, may be helpful. If the child is obviously frightened, the suggestions given below in the section on special fears can be tried.

THE USE OF MEDICATION

When tantrums and aggressive behaviour are severe, frequent, prolonged and the cause cannot be identified and removed, medication may be considered as a last resort. The drugs used to influence behaviour can be classified into groups with different types of effects. Some are intended to 'tranquillize', that is, to calm and quieten by reducing responses to environmental stimuli. There are sub-groups in this category that achieve their effects through different kinds of biochemical actions.

In some people, disturbed behaviour seems to be due to high anxiety. Sedatives or tranquillizers may help or a beta-blocker can be tried. The latter are drugs that are also used to treat high blood pressure. They act on the 'autonomic' nervous system that controls heart rate, blood pressure, respiration and other systems that support life without needing conscious control. The beta-blockers are sometimes helpful in reducing anxiety and thereby producing calmer behaviour, especially when disturbed behaviour is accompanied by rapid pulse, sweating, large pupils and a general impression of agitation. Many beta-blockers, some more than others, can precipitate an attack of asthma in children or adults who are susceptible. This possibility has to be considered very carefully before a beta-blocker is prescribed.

Occasionally, episodes of disturbed behaviour are related in some way to epilepsy and anti-epileptic medication proves helpful. In adolescents and adults, the cause of the disturbed behaviour may be an underlying abnormality of mood, giving rise to depression or manic excitement, in which case drugs to treat depression or mania or alternations of these can be given. If other psychiatric conditions are present (see Chapter 14) these also may be treatable with appropriate medication.

It is difficult to predict the effect of any particular medication in people with autistic disorders. There are some general guidelines for deciding which drug to try but it is always a matter of trial and error. Individuals may improve, there may be no effect or, occasionally, there can be adverse effects, either severe side-effects or a worsening of behaviour. For these reasons, if medication is given, the effects should be closely monitored.

Among the medications that may be given to people with autistic disorders to lessen overactive or disturbed behaviour there are some that make the skin sensitive to sunlight. This may cause swelling and a rash if the child spends any time in the sunshine. In any case, the harmful effects for anyone of exposure to sunlight are now well-known. Sun-blocking creams, clothing to cover arms and legs and shady hats are sensible measures. Parents should ask the doctor who prescribes any medication about light sensitivity and any other possible side-effects, so that appropriate precautions can be taken.

Since medication in autistic disorders is not in any sense curative of the underlying impairments and acts only on aspects of behaviour, it is preferable to use environmental and behavioural methods. This is particularly the case with children because their brains and nervous systems are still developing and the long-term effects of altering brain biochemistry in an immature central nervous system are not known. If medication is given, the dose should be as low as possible. If there is no effect or an adverse effect, the medication should be stopped or, if medically necessary, gradually withdrawn. Environmental and behavioural methods should always be used together with any medication.

Destructiveness and interference with others' possessions

This is a serious problem for many parents. The children, especially when still at a low level of development, cannot play constructively, so they often occupy themselves by examining the simple properties of the things around them. They soon discover that paper, including books and wallpaper, can be torn and that many hard things make a noise when hurled to the floor and an even more satisfying noise when they break. One small boy developed an unerring aim with his toy bricks and shattered all the light bulbs in his house. At a later stage, the children develop enough to want to fit one object inside another. They often do not comprehend that large into small won't go, so they try force to achieve their aim, perhaps having a temper tantrum from frustration at the same time. The products of excretion are easily available so smearing the walls may be added to the rest of the damage. They may wander round the house, turning things out of cupboards and scattering them around the floor, leaving a trail of chaos for others to clear up.

While this stage lasts, the same precautions have to be taken as for an active toddler. Things that are to be preserved, such as ornaments, or are dangerous, such as matches, have to be kept out of reach. Unbreakable crockery can be used and the best china put away. The kitchen may have to be locked if no one is in there to prevent accidents. Siblings, and parents as well, need somewhere where their special possessions are safe from the child. Precautions have to be taken to ensure that the child does not go uninvited into other people's houses.

Night-time may be a special problem. The child's bedroom should be safe and easily cleaned. If the child tears the wallpaper one night when you are asleep, there is not a lot of point in replacing it until this stage is passed. It is better to use a non-toxic washable paint that cannot be torn away.

Constant supervision is required at this stage of development. This can be exhausting if there is no relief. It may be possible for parents to share the burden to some extent or relatives may be able to help. Respite care on a regular basis, if the child accepts this without distress, can make things easier for the whole family.

The problems become less if and when the stage is reached at which more constructive activities can be introduced. If communication and understanding improve, the children can be taught that certain possessions are theirs but others are not and must not be touched. A set phrase to indicate ownership may help. One girl, around the age of seven years, was taught to point to objects and say 'That belongs to . . .' She took delight in saying, 'That belongs to Jenny' (her name), 'That belongs to Daddy' and so on. This was made into a game in which a member of the family would touch something and say 'That belongs to . . .' giving the wrong name. Jenny would then laugh with delight at the deliberate mistake and name the correct owner. She enjoyed this game and it gave her a better grasp of the concept of ownership.

Self-injury

Self-injurious behaviour, varying from mild to very severe, can occur in autistic disorders. The most severe and long-lasting self-injury occurs mostly in those with severe or profound levels of disability.

Minor forms of potentially self-injuring behaviour are common in children with autistic disorders in association with temper tantrums. Biting the back of the hand and head banging are particularly frequent when the children are angry or upset. Coping with the tantrums helps to reduce this behaviour.

Some children develop repetitive self-injurious behaviour that is not confined to temper tantrums and continues for long periods of time. This can take many different forms, including biting, scratching and head banging. The effects vary in severity from trivial to extremely severe. Behaviour such as regurgitating food, drinking excessive quantities of fluid, self-induced vomiting and poking fingers into body orifices can also be classed as self-injury.

Psychologists investigating self-injury suggest a number of inter-linked causes that keep the behaviour going even if they do not explain why it began in the first place. First, internal biological factors such as biochemical abnormalities may play a part in some cases. There are chemicals called opiates, resembling morphine, that occur naturally in the body. These reduce the feeling of pain and increase the feeling of well-being. Some of these chemicals are released in response to injury, so one theory is that self-injury is a way of increasing the level of opiates in the body and thus increasing the feeling of well-being. Second, the sensations produced by the self-injury may be experienced as interesting, especially if biochemical factors reduce pain sensations. Third, environmental factors, especially the interaction with carers, are very important; for example, self-injury may be a way of obtaining a carer's attention or it may be a way of avoiding too high demands. Self-injurious behaviour is most frequent in children who have little or no means of communication. In children with autistic disorders, the typical repetitiveness of the behaviour pattern is another factor tending to make self-injury long lasting.

Psychologists concerned with treatment of self-injury emphasize the importance of finding, if possible, the function or functions of the behaviour for the child or adult concerned. This is known as 'functional analysis' and is done by careful observation and recording of the situations in which the behaviour occurs. There are usually so many events during the course of any day that making records and selecting the crucial items is difficult. Computer technology is being developed to improve accuracy and make the task easier. With this information, the environment and the daily programme can be planned to minimize the occurrence of self-injury. One promising approach, once the function of self-injury has been determined for an individual, is to teach other, more appropriate, behaviour to achieve the same goal or goals as the self-injury. In children with little or no means of communication, teaching ways of indicating their needs and wishes seems likely to be a way of preventing self-injury before it begins.

Protective clothing has been used to prevent serious injuries. This is best avoided if possible because the devices used tend to restrict movements so that engaging in other activities is difficult or impossible. Also, the child or adult may start to self-injure in order to have the protection put on. If it has to be used, the time for which the special clothing is worn should be kept as short as possible. Various types of medication have also been tried. The only drugs that do seem to help in some cases are those that act against the natural opiate chemicals in the body. The opiate blockers reduce these levels so that the self-injury does cause pain. There are complicated ethical problems associated with this method. Even if protective clothing or medication is necessary as a short-term measure, they should be combined with functional analysis followed by behavioural methods based on the findings.

Chronic severe self-injury is one of the most distressing and difficult problems with which parents and carers have to cope. Advice should be sought, as early as possible, from psychologists with a special interest and experience in the field.

As with any type of behaviour problem in autistic disorders, self-injury can be a sign of discomfort, pain or illness so this possibility should always be considered if the behaviour newly appears or there is a marked change in the behavioural pattern. There are also a few congenital conditions in which self-injury is likely to occur, so medical examination is needed to see if any of these are present as well as the autistic disorder.

A review of recent advances in assessment and intervention has been written by Chris Oliver – see the reading list.

Restlessness and hyperactivity

Most young children with autistic disorders are restless, often wandering around aimlessly. The great majority are not truly hyperactive and do not move about much more than most other children of the same age. They appear hyperactive because they have a short attention span and the consequences of their actions are undesirable from the adult point of view. They are either purposeless and randomly interfering or else are pursuing their repetitive routines regardless of anyone or anything else. This type of restless activity tends to reduce if a structured programme for each day is organized and more constructive activities encouraged (see Chapter 11).

There are a small number of children with autistic disorders who do have the additional problem of an attention deficit and hyperactive disorder. This combination of problems is particularly difficult to cope with in a family home. The same psychological approaches that help other children with autistic disorders are appropriate but may produce little result. In children of this kind, medication such as methylphenidate (Ritalin) may prove helpful in reducing activity level and improving attention while it is working. Although there can be undesirable side-effects these are unusual. If it is going to be effective, the results are seen immediately. If it does not work it should be discontinued without delay. Because it has been misused as a stimulant drug, this medication should be prescribed under the supervision of a physician specializing in behavioural disorders.

Socially embarrassing behaviour

All young children are liable to cause embarrassment to their parents in public from time to time, providing many funny stories to be laughed at in retrospect. Children with autistic disorders do similar things, but they do them more often, they go on doing them for much longer and they do them with a total lack of inhibition.

With those whose comprehension of social rules is at a low level, anticipation of possible problems is essential. Shopping expeditions provide many opportunities for embarrassing behaviour, such as knocking down a huge display of tins in a supermarket, or grabbing bars of chocolate at the check-out. The young children have no idea of psychological barriers and will wander behind counters and into the back premises of shops quite unconcerned. Some of them run away at any opportunity, pursuing a straight course at considerable speed, heedless of all obstacles.

A small child may be willing to sit in the supermarket trolley or stay in a pushchair but they soon grow too big for these measures. The child can be encouraged to hold a basket and eventually to push the trolley. A consistent, patient approach and constant repetition is needed to develop positive behaviour in shops in place of disruption. When an action has to be prevented, it is better to give an instruction for alternative behaviour than to say 'No' or 'Don't do that'. For example, a calm but firm command to 'Hold my hand' combined with taking the child's hand can forestall the act of grabbing something from the shelves.

Visits to shops should, if at all possible, be planned so that they are short and at times when few people are around, until the child is more able to cooperate. It is easier to cope with the shopping and to try to teach appropriate behaviour if two adults are involved. Close supervision and the prevention of any inappropriate behaviour can be the task of one while the other collects the shopping. Among other advantages, one adult can take the child out of the store to avoid a long queue at the check-out, the point at which any child, let alone one with an autistic disorder, may behave inappropriately.

Particular social problems arise with those who can talk well. The children's habit of echoing words and phrases they have heard in the past can lead to unfortunate consequences. Parents have to be especially careful of the things they say in front of their child if they do not want them repeated in an exact copy of their accents and tone of voice. Swearwords are particularly easy to learn because the emphasis and intensity usually accompanying them catch the attention even of a child with little speech and poor comprehension. Naive remarks about other people, made in a loud voice, have to be discouraged.

The older children's lack of appreciation of social taboos often leads to problems. Removing clothes or passing urine in public may be done in all innocence by an adolescent or young adult. Parents and teachers have to lay down a series of rules in an attempt to forestall or prevent a repetition of such incidents. The trouble is that no-one can think of everything that might happen and life seems too short to teach the correct response in every imaginable situation, let alone the unimaginable ones that seem to crop up just as often. One can only do what one can and hope for the best. Once a rule is learnt, an autistic child tends to keep it under all circumstances. This leads to problems too, as with the child who learnt that one must always urinate in a lavatory and then suffered intense discomfort on a long drive in the countryside because he could not be persuaded to break the rule in this special situation. It is important to remember to show pleasure and appreciation when an outing has passed without a mishap.

Carol Gray has developed a method of encouraging appropriate social behaviour through 'social stories', written in words and pictures for the individual child, incorporating information and tactfully phrased instructions geared to their level of understanding and their special interests. This is a way of translating social rules into visible form and can be helpful for children with the ability to understand the simple stories. The method would be applicable to adults as well as children.

The consequences of a child's inappropriate behaviour can be more serious for the parents than simple embarrassment. Occasionally, a child with an autistic disorder has repetitive behaviour or speech that appears to have a sexual content. They can hear things from other children and repeat them in all innocence. One child, for example, sat through a sex education class at school and then constantly repeated the half-understood words and phrases regardless of where she was. This led to an investigation of possible sexual abuse, to the distress of the parents. In other cases, parents have been suspected of physical abuse because their child frequently shouts out angry, scolding words.

It is, of course, possible for children with autistic disorders to be abused in all kinds of ways but a high level of knowledge and experience of autistic conditions is required to assess each situation and to reach a proper conclusion. The content of repetitive speech or behaviour on their own is a very poor guide to the home life of the child. Why the children latch on to obscenities and angry words and tones of voice no-one knows. It is a fact that many do this once they have started school and met other children with colourful vocabularies. In this situation it is helpful to both the parents and the professionals involved to seek advice from someone with specialized experience in the field of autistic disorders.

Special fears

Some of the children are always tense and fearful and many develop fears of harmless things at some time or other. It is usually difficult to know the origin of the fears, but sometimes it is possible to trace then back to their beginnings. One little girl had a pair of new shoes that were uncomfortable because they rubbed her heels. From then on she screamed and refused to walk if shoes were put on her feet. After a time, she began to scream even at the sight of her shoes or slippers. A small boy put his finger into a bath of water that was a little too hot and could not be persuaded to enter the bath for years after that, although he was quite happy to sit in the large kitchen sink. Children who are developing normally may have experiences that alarm them when they are small, but usually they can communicate their fears to their parents and accept verbal reassurance and explanation. Children with autistic disorders have no way of asking for help and unexpected or distressing events tend to confirm their fears of the world and their dislike of any change.

The behaviour that was first caused by fear may continue as a routine habit long after the fear has gone. In this case it can be dealt with in the same way as other routines. Before this stage is reached the problem is more difficult to solve because the child's terror is so obvious and parents feel acute distress if they try to force the child into such frightening situations.

The most helpful approach is very gradual exposure to the frightening situation, known in the psychological jargon as 'desensitization'. It works best if each exposure is accompanied by something the child does enjoy. For example, the little girl who would not wear shoes was helped in the following way. At the time she loved to eat boiled eggs. When she had her egg for tea, a pair of slippers in her favourite colour was placed beside her while she was eating and taken away before she had finished. Without the egg the slippers produced screams, but with the egg they were accepted calmly. The time with the slippers was lengthened until the stage was reached when they could be put on her feet while she was eating. The time with slippers on was again lengthened until she wore them cheerfully all through tea. After this, her outdoor shoes were tried and these produced no fearful reaction. She wore them without any fuss and from then on they were put on in the morning in the usual way. The fear never recurred and buying new shoes is now looked forward to as a pleasant occasion.

It is not always possible to carry out this kind of plan. Chocolate sweets were tried for James, the little boy who was afraid of the bathtub, but the fear was too strong to be soothed by the sweets. It is interesting that this problem was eventually overcome in a different and unexpected way. Maria, a girl living *au pair* with the family and who was good with children, popped him into a bath on the first day she arrived, unaware of his fear. His astonished mother heard happy giggles and splashes and found her child enjoying his first bath in years as if he had one every day. Encouraged by her success, Maria persuaded James to use the lavatory, of which he had previously been afraid. In this case, it seems that the child was helped by the fact that Maria was not anticipating fear, whereas his parents had grown accustomed to it. They also learnt from the experience and were much more confident and successful in dealing with other, similar problems that occurred after this incident. It is interesting that Maria, who arrived knowing hardly any English, developed a close rapport with James because, as she explained, they both had a language problem and both were, so to speak, strangers in a strange land.

Another approach to fear of having a bath can be tried with children who are worried about the water, not the bathtub itself. The child is placed in the empty bath, perhaps in a swim suit if swimming is enjoyed, with some favourite waterproof toys. After a few sessions of this, a small amount of water is introduced. If this is accepted, then the amount of water is gradually increased, day by day, until the child accepts enough for a bath. The important point about desensitization is that each step should cause no anxiety. Care has to be taken to ensure that the triggers for fear are identified and that the whole sequence of steps is organized to deal with these. For example, if undressing in the bathroom sets off a panic attack, the plan would have to be modified to take account of this. If it is the sound of the water entering or leaving the bath, the problem might be solved if the tub is always filled and emptied when the child is well out of earshot.

As mentioned previously, some of the children are terrified of hair care, especially having hair cut. This is a difficult problem to deal with. Occasionally a child is so frightened that the hair is not cut for years, or attempts are made to cut it while the child is asleep. Taking a child to a hairdressing salon can be a nightmare, so some parents arrange for a hairdresser to come to their home. Techniques of distraction can be tried but are less likely to succeed where there is great fear. One variation of the distraction method is to keep something, such as a particular object, toy or food which the child likes very much, to be produced only during hair cutting if the child is cooperative. It can happen that a child accepts hair cutting without protest if accompanied by someone other than the parents, so this is worth trying, perhaps with the help of someone from the child's school.

Some families have dealt with their child's fear of dogs by buying a small puppy. This usually, though not always, works well. It is wise to choose a dog from a reputable breeder and of a type that is likely to be placid and good with children when grown up. This solution is not to be recommended unless the parents are fond of dogs and know exactly what care of a pet entails. They should also arrange in advance a possible alternative home for the puppy in case the child's fear of dogs does not improve.

Children with autistic disorders can develop a whole range of fears because of their sensitivity to loud noises, bright lights or other sensations. This may lie behind fears of, for example, aeroplanes, trains, motor-bikes, barking dogs and photographers' flash lights, or putting on clothes made of rough material. They find these stimuli painful and are not making a fuss about nothing. Calm reassurance and distraction of the child's attention may help if the sensitivity is not too severe. If it causes much distress, especially if it interferes with everyday activities, gradual desensitization can be very effective. Some clinical psychologists are particularly interested in these types of problems and parents can seek their help in working out a programme.

It can happen that a child overcomes a fear through a chance event. A girl liked to jump up and down in the water at the seaside but would scream if anyone tried to hold her with her feet off the bottom. One day she accidentally tripped and lost her footing but found that she was able to float with her special arm bands and swimming ring. From that moment she was utterly without fear of the sea and, in fact, became rather too confident for safety. Parents may be tempted to try the method of instant exposure to a feared situation but it can fail and intensify the fear. The method of gradual desensitization is much safer and surer.

Lack of fear of real dangers

This is the opposite side of the picture to the children's special fears, but can be equally worrying. Total lack of road sense is almost universal in the children. The children who like climbing tend to have at least one heart-stopping feat to their credit, such as walking along a narrow ledge on the roof or hanging out of the window practically by their toes. They are usually so sure-footed that no harm results, but there have been a very few instances in which children have been injured or killed because they were oblivious of real danger.

Parents have to be aware of this. They can teach the rules for crossing the road, avoiding fires, electricity and gas, and warn of other common dangers, but even the brightest of the children will learn these by rote and may not apply them to a new situation. All possible sources of danger both inside and outside the house have to be considered and proper precautions organized.

Stereotyped movements

The repetitive bodily movements that are so common in children with autistic disorders are not disruptive for other people but they do look strange and attract attention and criticism in public especially in an older child or adult.

The movements tend to diminish or cease when the child is

involved with some more constructive activity, especially if this requires movements that are incompatible with the stereotypies. This is why they are much less in evidence in a well-run classroom at school than they are in the playground in unstructured break times. One useful strategy for parents when out in public is to give the child something to carry, such as a shopping bag, or the supermarket trolley to push. Holding hands with someone else also helps, if the child will accept this.

It is not possible or desirable to try to suppress the movements completely. Attempts to do so lead to a build-up of tension and distress. Some very able adults have described how they feel the need to engage in their stereotyped movements at some time each day. The eventual aim is to diminish or stop them in public or when they interfere with other activities but allow them in privacy at specific times. This aim can be achieved for many people with autistic disorders but, for those with the most severe disabilities, it may not be possible to make much difference to their stereotypies.

Problems with eating

Eating problems are common in the early years. At least two different factors may be involved in feeding problems and food fads. First, some children with autistic disorders have trouble with controlling the movements of the muscles involved with chewing and swallowing. They are difficult to wean because they do not know how to cope with lumpy food. It is interesting to note that children born with severe visual combined with severe hearing impairments also often reject lumpy food. Food that needs chewing has to be introduced slowly, so that the child can practise without being frightened by lumps that are too big or hard to manage. One mother found that she had to teach her son to chew by moving his lower jaw with her hands to give him an idea of the movements required. Speech therapists have developed a series of exercises designed to help children who have trouble in coordinating tongue and mouth movements. These include, for example, blowing bubbles, blowing pieces of cotton wool and retrieving sweet food placed on the lips outside the mouth by using the tip of the tongue.

The second major reason for feeding problems arises from the children's resistance to change and their tendency to cling to special routines. Minor eating problems of this type can be dealt with by providing a good mixed diet, giving food only at meal-times and adopting an attitude of casual indifference to how much is eaten. If the child takes in adequate quantities of essential nutrients and fluid, it does not matter if, for example, they refuse certain kinds of food, or eat only one meal a day. In this situation, there is no need for a mother to cook special food for the child – perhaps because the rest of the family likes carrots and the child with autism never touches them. Children can miss a meal occasionally without coming to any harm and they are more likely to come round to trying something new if they are hungry and know they will get nothing else.

A number of the children go through phases in which their diet is restricted to a very few foods, for example, hamburgers and chips, or cereals and bread and butter cut into pieces of a precise size and shape. Usually, the foods they will eat are those that do not require lengthy chewing. Parents sometimes try to change the child's eating routine by allowing them to miss one or two meals in the hope that hunger will persuade them to eat more types of food. Occasionally this works but, much more often, the child seems indifferent to hunger and can last without food much longer than the parents are prepared to withhold meals. Providing that the child will eat some things, it is surprising how active and healthy almost all of them remain on the diets they choose.

It is, as always, important to remain outwardly calm and to show no anxiety about meals. This is a reasonable attitude considering how little the children's peculiar diets affect their health or even their weight. One tactic that sometimes helps is to provide the food the child will eat but to add a tiny quantity of some other food, preferably of a kind that is not noticeably different in appearance. If this is accepted, the quantity can be increased gradually and then other foods added. However, some children notice the added food at once and refuse to eat any of the meal, so the method will not work for them. Usually, the restricted diets are a passing phase, though they can last for years. The problem may disappear when the child starts school and has school meals, although some retain their special diet at home while eating a wide range of foods at school and elsewhere.

Some of the children will not eat with others but may eat if given meals on their own. Some will take food left for them if they are allowed to eat while moving around. For some, the texture of the food is the crucial factor as, for example, the child who will eat only uncooked, crunchy vegetables and fruit. The immediate problem of eating sufficient food can be solved by observing what, where and when the child will eat and fitting in with these idiosyncrasies. The longer-term problem of encouraging more conventional eating patterns has to be approached gradually and may need an individualized programme designed by a psychologist with experience in this field.

Most of the children will drink fluids even if they eat only a few foods. If needed, protein and vitamin supplements can be given in flavoured liquids.

There have been a very few cases of children who will eat nothing at all or who eat so little that their health is at risk. In such cases, medical and psychological help is required. There are one or two centres in hospitals that have a special interest in feeding problems where advice on treatment can be obtained.

If a feeding problem starts in a child who has previously eaten reasonably well the parents should make sure that the child does not have some physical illness, such as a fever or a painful mouth or throat, that has caused the loss of appetite.

The Principals' Group of the National and Local Autistic Societies has produced a helpful booklet on all kinds of problems associated with feeding – see the reading list.

Problems with sleeping

Some children with autistic disorders sleep well but others are poor sleepers. They may resist going to bed, lie awake once they are in bed, wake in the night and laugh, sing and, if they have speech, talk to themselves, wander round the house or get into their parents' bed, wake very early and refuse to go back to sleep, or any combination of these. Some have very little sleep at all and some seem never to have adjusted to the usual cycle of waking and sleeping.

Medication for inducing sleep may be helpful but it should be used only as a temporary measure. Some children are resistant and need a larger than usual dose, which should only be given on medical advice. For some, medication has the opposite effect to that intended and makes the child more active and irritable. It is very possible that new drugs with more specific effects on the physiology of sleeping will become available so it is worthwhile for parents to ask from time to time about the latest developments in this field.

A behavioural approach devised by specialist psychologists may work well. Briefly, the aim is to ensure that the child remains in bed, or at least in the bedroom, during the night. The child is put to bed at a reasonable time and then, whenever he or she gets up and leaves the bedroom, the parent returns the child to bed without any fuss, remaining with the child for as short a time as possible. Similarly, if the child wakes in distress and cries or screams, the parent should use any soothing tactics that work in the bedroom and not take the child downstairs or into the parents' own bed. If the child will not sleep without a parent in the room, the plan is for the parent to move a little farther away from the child each night or every few nights until finally she or he is outside the room. The process may take a long time but, if successful, the effort is worthwhile. It helps if the parents take turns to be on night duty so that each has some sleep.

There is, unfortunately, no guarantee of success. These problems tend to be most severe in the pre-school years and may improve spontaneously once the child goes to school each day. Regular physical exercise may also help.

Quiet, withdrawn children

So far I have described the behaviour of the children with autistic disorders who are active and react to their disabilities with a kind of angry determination. There are other children, a small minority, who respond in a different way. They are quiet and withdrawn, tending to isolate themselves from the world, rather than hitting their heads against it in rage and frustration. They may be unchildlike in their neatness and cleanliness, because they never explore their environment and have no interest in mud, sand or water. In contrast to the active child who climbs to the top shelf of the cupboard to reach forbidden objects and undoes locks in a way that Houdini would have envied, the passive children may do nothing for themselves. They give the impression that their hands lack the strength even to lift a spoon to their mouths, or to handle a toy that is placed in front of them.

This kind of child is less difficult to live with than those who are full of energy, but they tend to be even more detached and indifferent to affection. The book *The Siege*, written by Clara Claiborne Park, who is a parent of a child of this kind, gives an excellent and moving description of the way in which she helped her daughter, together with much detailed advice that other parents can follow. Despite her remoteness as a small child, Clara's daughter gradually emerged from this and developed a range of abilities, including remarkable skill with numbers.

Children of this kind, because they are quiet and gentle, may not be recognized as having a disorder in the autistic continuum and may be expected to fit into mainstream education with little or no special provision. At adolescence, some become disturbed and difficult in stark contrast to their amiability in childhood. The nature of their problems then becomes much more obvious. If the diagnosis is made when the child is young, the possibility of problems in adolescence can be anticipated and to some extent avoided by providing appropriate education and help from early childhood.

·11·

Teaching basic skills

Before 1971, when an Act of Parliament was passed giving all children, including those with disabilities, the legal right to be educated in school, many of those with autistic disorders were excluded from the educational system. Some parents in those days undertook the task of teaching schoolwork to their own children. Now, the children can attend school and parents do not have to take on the dual role. However, learning the basic skills of life begins in the home. Parents of children with autistic disorders often have a hard time trying to help them develop these skills. Some suggestions based on practical experience will, I hope, be of help.

General principles

The suggestions are only of use if they are applied with a full understanding of the level and pattern of abilities and disabilities of each individual child. A good level of skill in one area does not mean an equally good level in another. Pressing someone with an autistic disorder to attempt a task beyond their ability is a sure way of inducing inappropriate behaviour. On the other hand, no progress is made unless new things are tried. Parents and teachers have to tread a narrow line between too many demands and too few. Parents develop a deep knowledge of their own child while teachers develop a broad knowledge of many children. Cooperation between the two is the ideal.

A number of rules based on theories of how people learn are particularly relevant to teaching new skills. These are as follows – the first two were also mentioned in Chapter 10.

1 Behaviour that is rewarded is more likely to be repeated than behaviour that is not rewarded. As has already been emphasized, the problem is to find what does reward any individual child with an autistic disorder. Music, pleasant sensory stimuli and social attention if this is enjoyed by the child may be successful. Objects, activities or special interests that are part of the child's repetitive routines can be very effective as incentives and experience has shown that they can be used without leading to other problems.

2 Timing of the reward is important so that the child connects it with the behaviour.

3 New skills are learned more easily if they are broken down into small, easy steps. Children with autistic disorders are especially liable to be upset by failure, so making sure that the child can succeed at each small stage is important.

4 With some tasks, it is best to begin with the last step, then the next to last, and so on, so that the child is aware of completing a task successfully. This is called 'backward chaining'. Examples will be give later.

5 Prompts that help the child to succeed should be given at first and then gradually made less obvious ('faded') as the child learns the task, until prompts are no longer needed.

6 When trying to encourage the development of a new skill, or to change a behaviour pattern, the child should be asked to perform the new activity for a very brief time at first and allowed to stop *before* they become bored and restless or, worse, have a temper tantrum. The time can be extended very gradually.

7 The tendency to repetition of actions previously performed,

despite the many problems associated with it, can be used to good effect in teaching. The difficulty lies in finding ways to encourage the performance of a new action in the first place.

The pattern of skill development

The children often make very slow progress, or none at all for months or years. This is disappointing and frustrating for parents. However, children with autistic disorders typically have an unusual type of 'learning curve'. This means that, instead of making steady progress, however slow, they tend to learn something, then stick at this point for a long time – they reach a 'plateau' in the jargon. Then, when everyone has given up hope, they suddenly take a step forward. Sometimes they appear to learn something without preliminary practice. There are many examples, such as the boy of nine who tied his own shoelaces one day after his mother had tied them for him every morning up to that time. A girl refused to try to ride a bicycle, then, at the age of 12, she took her bike out of the shed and rode it competently round the garden. Sometimes there is an obvious reason for the change but often no explanation can be found. The special skills mentioned in Chapter 4, such as drawing, numerical or calendar calculations, that are found in perhaps one in 10 children with autistic disorders, usually emerge more or less fully formed, without previous practice.

Occasionally a child will perform a new skill once only and it may be many years before they try again. It is realistic to expect a slow rate of progress, on a different time-scale from that of most children. Most, however, do make at least some progress in acquisition of skills and this can continue into adult life.

Encouraging cooperation

Children with autistic disorders have no innate desire to please anyone else or to accept authority. The language difficulties limit comprehension of instructions and lead to confusion about what is required. In addition, many children with autistic disorders are extremely distressed at any experience of failure and hate to be corrected if they make an error.

It is very easy to overestimate how much the children understand of what is said to them. Those with little or no speech rely on visual clues rather than the words they hear. The children who say a great deal but are using the store of words in their rote memory appear to understand far more than they really do. One of the effects of poor understanding is that the child may pick up and respond to only one or two words in a sentence. The words that mean something to them are usually the nouns and some verbs specifying actions. Other words that are crucial to the meaning of an instruction may be incomprehensible and therefore ignored. For many children with poor understanding, the word 'Don't' may be an irrelevant noise, so the instruction 'Don't touch the oven' may be misinterpreted as 'Touch oven', with disastrous consequences. This is one of the reasons why the children may appear to choose to act in negative ways. Parents and anyone living or working with a child or adult with an autistic disorder need always to be aware of the limits of their understanding and to adjust the words they use accordingly. Positive instructions, for example, are simpler and easier to understand than those given in negative terms.

Methods of teaching and ways of communicating have to be tailored to the child's level of understanding and ability to perform any skill. If the child's developmental level is too low for learning a particular task, the child is likely to react negatively if attempts to teach that skill are continued. It is important to begin at a low level, well within the child's capacity, so that they are rewarded by success. The rate at which difficulty is increased has to be determined according to the child's progress. If, after trying to teach a child, it becomes obvious that he or she is not ready for that particular task, it should be left for a while and then tried again. It requires considerable insight and judgement to decide at any particular stage if increased pressure will help a child to succeed, or if it will intensify confusion and anxiety. The patchiness of the profile of skills that is so common in autistic conditions makes it difficult to assess ability in any one area.

There is no easy answer to this problem and parents and teachers have to decide the best course of action in the light of their knowledge of and feeling for the child and their past experience. It helps to remain calm and confident and reassuring because the children are sensitive to the emotions of people who are involved with them. If it is felt the child can succeed, the parent or teacher must be firm and show that he has to try, but must not lose their temper. If the parent or teacher is mistaken they must accept defeat with good grace and not blame the child.

In the pre-school years, autistic children may show no reaction when spoken to and may even ignore the sound of their own name. If this is the case, it helps to link it very deliberately to situations that are enjoyed, such as mealtimes, drinks and snacks, getting ready for an outing, physical play. The child's name can be introduced into favourite songs, especially when holding and cuddling the child. It is also sensible not to use the child's name a great deal in situations where the child is not required to respond. Parents and teachers should, for instance, avoid discussing a child in their presence because, apart from other objections, this allows them to fall back into the habit of hearing their name spoken but ignoring it.

Dislike of physical contact, which usually affects gentle touch rather than hugging and rough-and-tumble play, can make a child even less willing to co-operate. Suggestions for reducing this have been given in Chapter 9.

Some children with autistic disorders, and adults too, hardly ever choose to sit down even when engaged in activities such as eating, watching videos or listening to music. Many never learn to sit for very long but can be encouraged to sit for meals if they are allowed their food only when sitting down at the table. As with most attempts to change behaviour, the gradual approach is the best. At first, the child should be expected to sit only while eating. If this works well, it may be possible slowly to increase the time at table. This approach is relevant only for the children who positively enjoy their food and will eat when sitting down.

If activities such as playing with musical or constructional toys, looking at picture books, making jigsaw puzzles, drawing and painting are enjoyed, the materials can be produced only when the child is sitting down. It is easier for a child to stay sitting if an adult sits with them and helps them to engage in the activities. The session should finish before the child becomes restless and can be followed by something more active. The time will be short at first but can be extended gradually.

It is difficult for children whose speech is mainly echolalia to express a preference if asked to choose between two or more items. In response to the question, 'Do you want an apple or an orange?', the child may repeat the whole sentence, or else echo the last word ('orange') even if it was the apple that was preferred. It is easier for them to make a choice if they can see the alternatives and touch the one they want. There is then the opportunity for the parent to say, for example, 'Apple please' while giving the apple, so that the child will echo this and, eventually, use the construction appropriately.

Many young autistic children develop the habit of saying 'No' automatically when asked if they want something. It is part of ordinary social interaction to ask, for example, 'Do you want some toast?', 'Do you want juice?', 'Do you want to go for a walk?'. At the stage when the child answers in the negative even if they do want whatever is on offer, it is best to make the decision for the child without asking. This may appear to be depriving the child of choice. The reality is that they deprive themselves as a result of their social and language impairments. The way to ensure that the wishes of the child are taken into account is for parents or carers to observe the reactions to whatever is chosen for them and to note them for future action.

When a skill is learnt, the child may repeat it again and again until its performance seems meaningless and may resist any attempt to move on to another task. The methods of dealing with repetitive routines described in Chapter 9 are helpful in this situation.

Even if all the rules for encouraging interest in developing skills are followed, many of the children vary markedly in their cooperativeness from one time to another. Parents often notice that their children seem to have good days and bad days. Sometimes they are more alert, more interested in the world and more willing to learn. At other times, perhaps even the next day, they are withdrawn, irritable and refuse to cooperate. Occasionally parents notice that their child's appearance is subtly different on the bad days, perhaps looking pale with dark circles round the eyes. The reasons for these variations are unknown but it is possible that they are due to cyclical physical changes. On a day when a child is clearly functioning less well than usual, it is best not to press them to do things they find difficult.

Toilet training

Some autistic children are toilet trained without any difficulty and some become clean and dry at an unusually early age. Others are late in learning and may resist any attempt to train them. The training methods that are used with other children may be successful with those who have autistic disorders but they require a high degree of patience and persistence. The general rule is not to make any fuss about the children's mistakes, but to put them on the pot or lavatory regularly and especially at the times when they are most likely to need to empty bowels or bladder. These are usually on waking after a dry night or daytime sleep, after meals and after drinks given between meals. Each child has to be observed carefully so that the time between eating or drinking and emptying bowels or bladder can be worked out fairly accurately. If successful, the child should be given lots of praise and attention, or some other suitable reward. If nothing happens, no emotion should be shown.

The trouble is that methods that work with other children are often no use at all with children with autistic disorders. Some of them seem to dislike or even fear the pot or lavatory. It is worthwhile trying to find out if they feel uncomfortable or insecure and if so, for what reason. Small pot-chairs can be bought that are stable and comfortable. An adult-size lavatory may be too high off the ground for a small child, so something to place his feet on will help. A very cold seat will be enough to worry some children. The flushing of the toilet may terrify some, though it can fascinate others.

Resistance to change in an established routine is one of the reasons for delay in toilet training. There are a number of children who will wet or soil or both only when wearing a nappy. They have excellent bowel and bladder control because they can remain clean and dry for hours until a nappy is put on them. As babies, they learnt to associate bowel and bladder function with wearing a nappy and cling to this routine after infancy has passed. One approach that may work is to try to change the routine gradually by putting a nappy on the child followed immediately by sitting them on the pot or lavatory. If the child accepts this, the nappy could be put on more loosely, then just draped over the pot or lavatory seat, then gradually reduced in size until it is no longer needed.

Self-care

This includes dressing, using knife, fork and spoon, washing, brushing and combing hair, cleaning teeth and all the other necessities of daily living. Children who are not disabled try to imitate these activities, which they see performed by other members of the family. When they are strong enough and well coordinated enough they begin to cooperate in the care given by their parents and soon want to take over these functions for themselves. They want to try washing, dressing and feeding themselves even if they make a mess in the process. Children with autistic disorders, on the other hand, may go through a phase, around one or two years of age, of actively resisting attempts to wash and dress them. Every item of daily care may precipitate a tantrum at this stage. Later on they tend to accept all these attentions passively. Having been cared for by others from birth they resist any change in the daily programme especially if some effort is demanded of them.

Young children with autistic disorders usually do not learn practical skills by being told how, nor by being shown how, but they may learn by direct experience. If a child is physically guided through the pattern of movements necessary for a particular skill the chances are that they will eventually be able to follow the pattern on their own. For example, a mother taught her little boy to fasten buttons as follows. She chose a garment with large buttons and easy buttonholes on the front. She stood behind the child and held his hands firmly but not too tightly so that she could guide them through the movements necessary for fastening the buttons. At first his fingers felt limp and his mother had to do all the work. After about a week, she began to feel some tension in his hands. Little by little he followed her movements until in the end he was fastening the buttons by himself. This type of teaching can be adapted for other self-care tasks and many kinds of physical activities.

It is also helpful to break tasks down into simple steps. It is often best to teach the last step first and work backwards so the child is always the one to finish the job – the process known as 'backward chaining'. For example, when learning to put on socks, the child is first taught to pull them up after the foot and heel are in place. When this is mastered, the next step is to pull the sock over the heel and so on.

Dressing is a special problem because it involves putting things on the right way out, the right way round and in the right sequence. If you consider all the operations involved in putting on a pullover with the seams inside and the V neck in front, you can see that it is a most complicated activity. Even when a child is able to put clothes on, they may still need to be taught how to put them on in the right order and the right way round. To start with, it will be necessary to place the clothes in front of the child in the correct order and arranged so that they will end up in the correct position and to give a guiding hand when necessary. Some children are helped by labels that indicate the inside and back of garments.

One difficulty is that autistic children do not have much conception of a finished result. They do not put the final touches to dressing, such as tucking shirt inside trousers, or pulling up the socks neatly. Hair tends to be brushed the requisite number of times without regard to the actual style in which it is supposed to be worn and without thinking about the back, which cannot be seen in a looking-glass. Face and hands may be washed with vigour, but without removing streaks of dirt on areas left untouched by the operation. They are often unaware of which clothes are suitable for the prevailing weather and will put on thick underclothes in the summer, or light T-shirts in the winter. Supervision and tactful assistance or verbal reminders are necessary. Such help should be given gently and pleasantly without any hint of criticism or nagging.

An interest in clothes and general appearance is a good thing to encourage. It is worthwhile taking extra trouble to dress the children so that they look as neat and attractive as possible. This is a help towards being accepted socially and also provides a reason for people to make nice remarks to the child. As they grow older, the children may begin to take some interest in their clothes and enjoy expeditions to buy new ones. This is a happy contrast to the early years when many autistic children furiously resist any attempt to try on garments in shops.

The children should be encouraged to feed themselves even if they are messy eaters. They may have to use only a spoon and fork for a long time. Some of them find problems in coordinating a knife and fork for cutting food as in the English method of eating and may manage better if allowed to adopt the American style of eating pre-cut food with a fork alone.

Helping in the home

Children with disabilities are dependent for so long and need so much special care that they tend to become passive members of their families. It is better for them if they have some positive role to play, however limited this may be. Laying the table with cutlery is one task that many can achieve and can be taught by physically guiding the child through the movements. Carrying out the task provides the opportunity for learning the names of the implements, counting the places to be laid and naming each person who will take part in the meal.

Clearing the table, putting out the milk bottles, carrying a small shopping bag, pushing a trolley in a supermarket, wheeling a small wheelbarrow in the garden are other examples of tasks that even young or very disabled children can take part in. Jobs that are quick to perform are best to start with. It is more difficult to persuade the children to persist at an endless task like clearing leaves from the garden lawn. They cannot understand the purpose and soon wander away. When they are older they may become better at such occupations.

If a task involves a sequence of operations, many of the children tend to forget the steps involved. One little girl of seven was helping in the garden by taking a basket full of weeds to the compost heap. She set off down the long garden path, then after a few yards she stopped and looked puzzled. Her father repeated the instructions, her face cleared and she set off again, only to stop once more. She finally reached the destination and disposed of the weeds, but had to have the separate instructions repeated four times altogether. After a while she had the whole task clear in her mind and could carry it out unaided.

Children who can say some words may be able to learn to take simple messages. These should at first relate to something that the child likes, such as letting someone know that a meal or a cup of tea is ready. If the child enjoys eating or drinking, they are likely to be willing to take such a message when they make a connection with the fact that they also will have the meal or a cup of tea. Depending on the child's level of ability, teaching may require a number of steps. The first is to practise saying the phrase, for example, 'Tea's ready, Mary'. Then the child can be lead to Mary, who is primed in advance, and prompted by a whisper to say the words. Mary then shows great pleasure, thanks the child and all go to have tea. Gradually the prompt should be faded, then the child taken only part of the way until they can take the message on their own. One problem in teaching a child with an autistic disorder to carry messages is their lack of understanding that words have to be heard by the recipient for them to have any effect. They tend to assume that speaking the words is sufficient regardless of where the other person is at the time. This is all part of their incomprehension of the purposes and methods of communication. This has to be taken into account when teaching.

Toys and games

The impairment of imagination severely limits the range of toys and games that children with autistic disorders can make use of and enjoy. They tend to prefer toys that involve visuo-spatial skills such as shape and colour matching, jigsaw puzzles or constructional materials. There is now a wide range of mechanical and electrical equipment for children that is attractive to many children with autistic disorders, especially those who are more able. Computers and computer games are particularly fascinating even to some who have few skills in other areas. This technology is being applied to the educational and leisure needs of children with disabilities including autistic disorders and it is well worth keeping up with the latest advances. The disadvantage is that computer activities can easily become a dominant obsession, so parents should, from the start, impose clear limits on the time allowed.

It is worth trying to engage the children in simple games. Singing games with actions are likely to be enjoyed. Most enjoy chasing games though they have difficulty in understanding the idea of taking turns to chase and be chased. They may learn to play hide and seek when they have sufficient understanding to know that objects still exist even if they are hidden away. It is best to begin by playing with one of the child's favourite possessions. One helper can cover the child's eyes or take them out of the room, while the other does the hiding. The child will need to be helped to search and the object will have to be 'found' quickly at first, to avoid causing upset through failure. As the child begins to see the point and to enjoy the surprise element, the game can go on longer and they can be encouraged to search for themselves. The child will tend to go back to the same place over and over again and will need cues to other possible hiding places. Most of the very simple games enjoyed by young children can be adapted to include a child with an autistic disorder. The experience is particularly valuable if other children can join in but they usually need adult guidance to help them adapt to the level of the child with an autistic disorder.

Some of the children reach the level at which they can play picture-matching games or board games such as ludo or snakes and ladders. Some of the most able learn to play chess and do well because of their excellent visuo-spatial memories. When young, most of the children have no concept of winning or losing and board games give the opportunity of teaching this. The trouble is, if and when they do learn, they may become very upset or angry and have a major temper tantrum if they lose. Board games at home with the family can be useful to teach at least a show of good grace when losing, if the nerves of everyone concerned can stand living through the learning process.

The hardest problem is to keep up the children's interest in any activity. Other children are eager to try out in play their developing understanding of the social and physical world. Children with autistic disorders lack this drive because they have no comprehension of what life is about. They need supervision and encouragement to prevent them filling all their time with their repetitive routines.

Physical activities

Since children with autistic disorders have little capacity for creative play, it is especially useful to encourage physical activities that are enjoyable without the need for imagination and understanding and use of language. Physical exercise is also reported to diminish inappropriate behaviour. Such activities are also helpful for improving the problems of motor coordination so often seen in autistic disorders.

The children usually enjoy listening and moving to music, walking and running, sand and water play, swings, roundabouts, slides and climbing frames. Many learn to swim even though they cannot take part in any other sport. Horse-riding supervised by qualified instructors who are experienced in working with disabled people often proves to be a special pleasure. If there is access to sessions in a gymnasium, they may enjoy using some of the apparatus, especially trampolines, and may achieve surprising levels of skill. Here too, qualified instructors must be present to supervise. Many eventually learn to ride tricycles or bicycles, with or without stabilizers. Most are happy when riding in cars or other forms of transport. Even adventurous pursuits such as rock-climbing may be attempted providing they are organized and supervised by instructors who are trained, experienced and understand the needs of people with autistic disorders. Some of the more able learn to play games that involve only two people, such as table-tennis.

Difficulties may arise in playgrounds open to any children. Those with autistic disorders may run straight into swings being used by other children without being aware of the danger. They may have no idea about taking turns and push other children out of the way or even off the equipment. When this behaviour is checked, there may be temper tantrums and screaming. It is important to be calm but adamant that difficult or dangerous behaviour will be prevented, if necessary by removing the child from the playground as soon as problems begin.

Poor motor coordination tends to reduce the children's opportunities for physical exercise. Some skills can be taught by helping the child physically to move hands, arms and legs appropriately. The guidance can be reduced bit by bit until it is no longer needed. Riding a tricycle, for example, can be taught in this way. Another problem can be fear that inhibits a child from trying some activities. The gradual desensitization approach as described in Chapter 10 can be used to overcome the anxiety.

Children with profound learning difficulties

Among the whole range of children with autistic disorders, there are some who have very severe or profound learning difficulties and whose capacity for progress is very limited. Their disabilities are shown by their lack of practical skills in everyday life and their poor performance on psychological testing. As with all children with autistic disorders, their real level of ability becomes clearer with increasing age and no firm decision should be made before five years old at least. There are occasional children who have one or two specific visuo-spatial skills, such as dexterity with jigsaw puzzles or who can chatter repetitively, but have no other skills at all. These children can be a puzzle because they appear to have more ability than is in fact the case. If psychological testing reveals consistently that they have profound learning difficulties, they also will need the type of programme to be described below.

Applying pressure to any of these children to make them perform tasks above their level of ability produces no useful result and may lead to temper tantrums, negativism, aggression towards others, or self-injury. An organised daily programme of activities in which they can participate is essential to help them enjoy a reasonable quality of life and to make life easier for the whole family.

The important skills for them to acquire, as far as they possibly can, are those of basic self-care, especially toilet training and self-feeding. These should be taught in very small steps, with gentle physical prompting, as a regular part of each day.

The types of leisure pursuits they can enjoy are the physical activities described above. Despite the children's very severe disabilities, some of them achieve surprising levels of skill in one or more of these activities, given patience and gentle persistence from the instructor.

The development of 'Snoezelen' rooms, with equipment that provides stimulation to the senses of sight, hearing, smell, touch, vibration and movement has been of benefit to children with severe impairments, including those with autistic disorders. The same kinds of activities, suitably modified for mature age and larger size, are appropriate for adults with profound learning difficulties.

Physical health

The children should be taught basic rules of hygiene, including teeth cleaning and care as far as they are able to learn. Those who are less able will need to be supervised in all health matters and the most disabled will need complete care.

As described in Chapter 10, those children who have problems with chewing or insist on a diet limited to sweet foods can be susceptible to gum disease and tooth decay. Careful and regular toothbrushing is essential. If the child will accept it, an electric toothbrush, if used properly, cleans effectively and also helps the child to become used to the feeling of vibration in the mouth, which is similar to that of some dental instruments. Regular visits to the dentist are necessary and should begin well before any treatment is needed.

Writers on health matters usually stress the importance of a balanced and varied diet. This rule can be difficult to apply to the many children with autistic disorders who eat only what they decide they will and generally show no symptoms of dietary deficiency, doubtless to the chagrin of the diet fanatics.

As already mentioned, physical exercise is helpful in many ways for children with autistic disorders, not least from the point of view of physical fitness.

Most of the children are active and energetic and have few illnesses. There are some who have various conditions due to allergies, including asthma. It has been suggested that allergies are a cause of autism but no firm evidence for this has been published. If the autistic disorder is associated with a physical disorder, such as tuberose sclerosis, appropriate treatment and supervision will be needed for this.

Epileptic fits occur in a substantial minority of people with autistic disorders. If they do appear, investigations are needed to search for any underlying physical cause. It is often appropriate not to start medication immediately but to have a period of observation, for example if the fits happen only with a fever, or if only one or two occur and no underlying cause or EEG abnormality is found. If medication to control recurrent fits is needed, there should be regular monitoring of its effectiveness and possible side-effects.

The problems of communication, especially expressing feelings, make it difficult for children with autistic disorders to indicate when they do not feel well, or to show the site of any pain. As described earlier, they can appear not to notice even severe pain. Parents often have to deduce that the child is unwell by observation of such behaviour as extra fretfulness, lack of appetite, lethargy, rashes or a feverish flush. This can occur even in more able children with good language. If the child has some speech, it is useful to teach a few words that can be used if they are in pain or discomfort. 'Throat sore' or 'Leg hurt', does give some guide to what is wrong. A small girl liked to have an adhesive plaster put on any minor injury. When she had an attack of tonsillitis the first sign was when she said to her mother, 'Poor froat – put plaster on.'

Many young autistic children furiously resist attempts at physical examination although some may happily accept medical procedures when they are older. Sometimes it can help the child to accept more easily if being examined is practised as part of a game with parents or siblings at home. This can include accustoming the child to the feeling of a cold stethoscope on the chest, using some similar sized metal object such as the end of a torch. It is also useful to practise opening and closing the eyes and the mouth when told. If possible, the child should get to know the family doctor as a friend before any treatment is needed so that there is less apprehension if the child does become ill. Unfortunately, the busy schedule of most family doctors means that this is hard to achieve.

If a child has to go into hospital it is usually better if a parent or other carer can accompany them. The child with an autistic disorder is likely to be very disturbed by being in a strange place and needs the reassurance of the presence of a familiar person. Any toys or objects that the child clings to should go as well. The doctors and nurses will need the parent's help to explain and give instructions in a way the child understands. The parent can also tell the staff of the child's needs since the children often cannot convey their meaning to strangers. The doctor and charge nurse may appreciate some information about children with autistic conditions if they have not treated a child of this kind before. In this situation parents have to hide their natural anxiety, present a calm and confident front to their child and cooperate fully with the medical and nursing staff, so that the child feels as happy and relaxed as possible. Despite their social and communication impairments, many children with autistic conditions are remarkably good at picking up small signs of unhappy emotions in other people.

A doctor or dentist who is treating a child should be told if they are receiving any medication of any kind. This is particularly important if an anaesthetic, local or general, has to be given. Children with autistic conditions may be muddled and confused when they wake up from an anaesthetic. They will be helped and comforted if a parent or another familiar person is there to give reassurance. Some children with autistic conditions are unusually resistant to sedatives, pre-medication or anaesthetics. In some cases these excite rather than sedate them. This possibility should be mentioned to medical or dental staff who are treating the child.

The uses and problems of medication were mentioned in Chapter 10. If medication is prescribed, parents should ask for detailed information about the reasons for prescribing, dosage, method of administration, when it should begin to act, possible side-effects, how to detect them and what to do if they occur, if there are special things to avoid, such as sunlight or particular foods, and how long the medication will be continued.

·12·

Babies with autistic spectrum disorders

Autistic disorders are usually not diagnosed until the age of two or later, so no-one can recommend well-tried methods of dealing with the problems in babies. If ever a reliable method of making a diagnosis in infancy is developed, it will then be possible to test ideas in practice. This chapter is included in case there are readers who suspect that a baby they know may have an autistic disorder, perhaps because of the behaviour pattern and a family history.

The interactions of babies with their parents should be a two-way process, with the baby contributing eagerness for and pleasure in response to the attention. This rewards the parents and helps to strengthen the mutual bonds. Babies who have autistic behaviour from birth tend not to show enjoyment of or even the need for social attention so the parents are not rewarded in the usual way for their efforts. It says much for the strength of parental feelings in human beings that most keep trying. It seems reasonable to suggest that, if a baby is undemanding or even rejecting of some forms of contact, the parents should observe the things that do seem to give pleasure and use these when caring or playing. Most such babies like active physical play such as tickling or bouncing up and down. They also usually love music, so singing or playing favourite tapes while dressing, washing, or changing can help the baby accept these procedures with less protest.

Many children with autistic disorders pay more attention to words that are sung to a tune than those that are spoken. The same seems likely to be true of the babies. Some show enjoyment if words are whispered into their ears – it may be the tickling sensation they like but, whatever the reason, it is a good idea to associate words with pleasurable feelings.

Parents often remember that fascination with particular stimuli, such as lights, television, a special sound or object, started during the first year of life. Some recall that the babies could be absorbed in these experiences for long periods of time. No one knows the long-term effect of either allowing this or preventing it. Again, it seems a sensible idea to compromise by allowing enjoyment of these activities for a time but then to intervene to try to involve the baby in more sociable play. The same goes for a baby who is content to be alone much of the time. The aim should be to make social interactions positively rewarding for the baby in whatever way can be found but to stop before boredom or resistance begins.

From parents' accounts, it appears that most babies who are later recognized to have an autistic disorder are quiet and undemanding. Babies who scream much of the time are in a minority. The hardest thing for parents of babies like this is that cuddling does not soothe and may even make things worse. Most discover that walking round, rocking and singing to the baby are helpful, as are the movements of a pram or a car. The problem is that the screaming starts again as soon as the movement stops and may go on through the night. There is no fund of advice that is guaranteed to be of help with such babies. Parents, especially if it is their first child, are often made to feel inadequate by others who criticize because they 'cannot manage the baby'. The critics would experience an equal lack of success if they tried to care for the child.

If the baby does not sleep and cries a great deal at night, sometimes music or some low continuous mechanical sound proves helpful. Leaving a light on or, conversely, excluding light may induce the baby to settle but none of these remedies is guaranteed to work. The degree of exhaustion experienced by the parents can be reduced if it is possible for them to take turns in coping or to involve someone else who is able to take a share of night care.

As with all other age groups, a regular, predictable routine for each day is the aim. This is relatively easy to achieve with the quiet babies but much more difficult with those who cry or scream a great deal and who are awake at night.

Adolescents and adults who remain dependent

Variations in the pattern of skills and behaviour are even wider among adolescents and adults than among children with autistic disorders. At one end of the scale, some change so little that they still have the same problems as those of the young child. At the other end, some adolescents have progressed so much that they are in mainstream education and are likely to become independent as adults. For these, the problems of adolescence have something in common with those of other teenagers as well as the special difficulties arising from the autistic impairments.

The special needs of those who are more able will be discussed in a later section. Here, the focus will be on those who remain dependent all their lives.

Adolescents

INAPPROPRIATE BEHAVIOUR

Many, though not all, of the more disabled adolescents show an exacerbation of difficult behaviour in the teenage years. The physiological changes that lead to puberty and increase in physical size also produce psychological changes. It seems that, even in those who are most severely disabled and unaware of social situations, adolescence brings a reluctance to accept adult authority and a determination not to give in. In those with limited ability, these feelings may be shown in a return to the temper tantrums, aggression and other behaviours of the early years. It is much harder for parents to cope with a tantrum in someone who is bigger and stronger than they are and is aware of the fact. Immature behaviour in a teenager also attracts more adverse reactions in public than the same behaviour in a small child.

Head-on confrontations are even less likely to produce useful results with an adolescent than they were with a child. Both at home and at school, careful planning is required. Just as in childhood, the programme for each day should be organized, predictable and presented in visual form. Within this framework, the activities and demands made on a teenager have to be adjusted to take into account the changes in age, interests and attitudes. It may be best, if it is possible, to avoid situations where problems are likely to occur.

EDUCATION

Pupils attending special schools can stay until they are 19 years of age. The educational programme should be planned to help develop skills that will be useful in adult life.

Cooperation between home and school in organizing activities and responding consistently to inappropriate behaviour is of great value. It may be that the behaviour is very different in the two environments. Usually, if there is a difference, the behaviour is calmer and more cooperative at school than at home but it can be the other way round. There is the temptation to blame those in charge where the difficulties occur but this is unjustifiable and unconstructive. An exchange of ideas and mutual support is much more helpful.

LEISURE ACTIVITIES

Inappropriate behaviour is always less likely when the individual is occupied. Teenagers with autistic disorders, like all young adults, tend to lose interest in the childish activities they enjoyed when younger. The problem is that those who are less able have no interest in the activities that fill the lives of other adults and cannot find constructive occupations for themselves. Parents and teachers have to explore all the possibilities for occupation and leisure that may be interesting and enjoyable to the individual concerned. Physical activities of all kinds are among the most likely to appeal. Computers may still hold their fascination and art work, pottery, weaving, gardening, domestic work and other practical occupations have all been enjoyed by some. The aim is to develop an atmosphere of cooperation and give and take that is appropriate for those who are becoming adults. At the same time, parents and teachers have to retain sufficient control to maintain the all-important structure for each day and to keep the teenager with an autistic disorder safe and in good health. Keeping the right balance is not an easy task.

SEXUAL DEVELOPMENT

Puberty is usually not delayed in children with autistic disorders, even though they often look younger than their actual age. Interest in the social aspects of sexual relationships requires more language and social understanding than is found in most of those teenagers with autistic disorders who will remain dependent all their lives. Some develop a curiosity about their own and other people's bodies and may try to touch and look in inappropriate ways or even try to undress other children. This should be stopped immediately but without any display of negative emotion. Most, sooner or later, discover for themselves how to masturbate. The rule must be that this is done only in private. Again, it is essential to react calmly, conveying the rule with clarity but without anger or distress. There has been some discussion among

parents and professionals as to the desirability of teaching someone with an autistic disorder to masturbate to orgasm if they are
showing signs of sexual arousal and do not seem to know how
to obtain relief. The problems associated with this and the emotional complications of embarking on such a programme are too
great for this to be advisable.

Menstruation usually begins within the same age range as with
other girls. Most seem to accept this without much concern.
Perhaps to a girl with an autistic disorder, it is just one more
inexplicable event in a puzzling world. A routine for changing
pads regularly should be followed with the aim of teaching the
girl eventually to cope for herself. Sometimes a teenager will talk
about her periods to people she meets. Although it is an excellent
idea to adopt an open and matter-of-fact attitude towards the
facts of life, it is necessary to teach discretion in these matters
because there are still many people who are shocked or embar-
rassed by these subjects. You can explain that the time to make
comments or ask questions is when alone with parents or other
carers and not when other people are around. As always, the
calm approach is essential.

Asking questions about conception and birth presupposes a
reasonable level of language development, so it is only a small
minority of the more dependent adolescents who will even ask
their parents about these matters. Answers should be frank, but
simple enough for the teenager's understanding and rules for
socially acceptable behaviour in these matters should be included
in the discussion.

Some adolescents with autistic disorders are naively friendly to
everyone and are easily led. Some girls are particularly likely to
approach men and may show physical affection indiscriminately.
Parents and other carers are properly concerned about the dangers
that could ensue. Most girls with autistic disorders who remain
highly dependent can be supervised closely enough to avoid problems of sexual encounters. However, if there is the possibility of
an undesirable contact occurring, the question of prescribing a
contraceptive pill or other contraceptive measure has to be considered. It must also be borne in mind that some teenage boys with
autistic disorders could be vulnerable to sexual abuse.

Adults

People with autistic disorders tend to look and behave much younger than their years. The concerns of adolescence continue long into adult life. Eventually, increasing age tends to bring calmer and more appropriate behaviour after the turmoil of adolescence, though it is not possible to say for any individual when this is likely to occur.

OCCUPATION

After school, it is essential for adults with autistic disorders to have regular, daily occupation. A few of those who are dependent on others are able to work at simple, routine jobs in paid employment. The great majority require sheltered work in day centres. As in all other aspects of life, the work available needs to be suitable for the abilities and interests and attention span of the individual, the daily timetable needs to be structured and clearly set out in visual terms and adequate help and supervision should be available from trained staff. The work environment should be calm, quiet and should provide enough personal space. This is particularly important for many people with autistic disorders. These are the ideal conditions. The types of centres that actually exist and the problems of obtaining a place are mentioned later (see Chapter 18).

LEAVING HOME

A small minority of children and adolescents with autistic disorders attend boarding school for the later part of their school life. Most go to day schools and live at home during their school-age years. Parents have to give careful thought to the question of where their children will live when they become adults. It is necessary to start thinking some years before the child becomes 18 years old, because good residential places are in short supply.

The placements that are available are discussed in Chapter 18.

Many parents find it difficult to think about the possibility of their children leaving home and being cared for by strangers. They know they understand their child better than anyone else and they worry endlessly about what will happen when their son or daughter no longer has the protection of home and family. Despite the emotional distress, parents need to face the fact that they will not always be able to care for their child. Their circumstances may change for all kinds of reasons, making it essential to find residential care for the person with an autistic disorder. The needs of sisters and brothers who are living at home, as well as the quality of life of the parents themselves, have to be considered. It is much better to plan in advance and, if possible, to see the person concerned settled into a home while the parents have health and strength to find the best placement and to take action if a particular home is chosen and then found to be unsuitable. Furthermore, the transition is eased if the parents can have their son or daughter home for weekends, frequently at first and then less often as they settle in.

From the point of view of the young adult with an autistic disorder, there are advantages in leaving home. This, after all, is the most usual pattern of life. They will meet different people, have access to new experiences at least some of which they will enjoy, they may learn new skills and more adaptive behaviour and be able to take part in a wider range of leisure activities. Often, but by no means always, there is a difficult period of settling in, which lasts for varying lengths of time. If the environment is right, this passes and life becomes easier and more enjoyable.

·14·

The more able children, adolescents and adults

Definition and diagnosis

I am including in this group the children, adolescents and adults who have language and non-verbal skills in the range from low average up to superior. The epidemiological study that was carried out in Sweden, as mentioned in Chapter 5, suggests that three to four in every 1000 children have this type of developmental disorder.

During infancy and early childhood, some of those who are more able show the behaviour pattern of typical autism. As they grow older, language and other skills develop well and they become more and more like the Asperger group. Others fit Asperger's descriptions of his syndrome from the beginning, having no delay in language or adaptive skills. Most, whatever their early history, by the time of adolescence or early adult life have most or all of the features described by Asperger, with repetitive speech and active but naive social interaction. A small minority retain more of the characteristics of Kanner's syndrome, being socially aloof and uncommunicative despite good comprehension and use of language on psychological testing. Yet others fit neither of these syndromes but have a mix of features though clearly being in the autistic continuum.

As explained in Chapter 3, the latest versions of the international classifications, ICD 10 and DSM IV, have as an essential criterion for Asperger's syndrome the absence of delay in development of language and other adaptive skills. In clinical practice, as distinct from research, it is the current pattern of behaviour that determines the needs of each individual, rather than the early history. It is more important to recognize that someone has an autistic continuum disorder and to assess their level and pattern of ability than to argue about which sub-group they belong to.

Childhood

The children who have typically autistic behaviour in their early years are likely to be recognized as having a developmental disorder even if the correct diagnosis is not made.)The problems and needs of those who begin to talk at the usual age and whose self-care and practical skills develop more or less normally are very often unrecognized until major problems occur at school. Many are not diagnosed until adolescence or adult life, if ever.

Early recognition of the nature of the children's disabilities is as necessary for those who are more able as it is for those with more severe disabilities. The more able children are impaired in their understanding of the nature of social interaction, are unable to use their good speech for true reciprocal communication and are rigid and repetitive in their imagination and their pattern of activities. They have the same basic impairments as the more severely affected children but manifest them in somewhat different ways. They also have the same need for a structured, organized programme and for a timetable to provide a framework for each day.

PROBLEMS AT HOME AND AT SCHOOL

There are some more able children who have a gentle, amenable temperament. Most, however, have an intense determination to do what they want to do regardless of any considerations. They are unconcerned about the consequences of their actions, whether they affect other people or themselves. This is probably due to an inability to foresee consequences, to weigh up the pros and cons and to make sensible plans for the future. The absence of these skills is very probably a direct consequence of the neuropathology that underlies autistic spectrum disorders.

The same single-mindedness often leads to difficulties at school. If a correct diagnosis has not been made, the child's stubborn refusal to do anything that does not interest them and their habit of saying exactly what they think can easily be interpreted as cheeky disobedience. They tend to be unpopular with other children because they do not share the interests of their age peers and are recognized as odd and different. The undiagnosed bright child with an autistic disorder can be intensely unhappy at school. Some do not know how to tell anyone of their misery and endure in silence. Some are aggressive to their peers who torment them and are then in further trouble. Some refuse to go to school and some, in adolescence, have a depressive reaction or other psychiatric illness.

Another characteristic that can cause difficulties at home and at school is the tendency to talk on and on about the same subject, or to ask repetitive questions regardless of the answers or, most irritating of all, to engage in arguments that are endless because the child always finds a new objection to whatever is suggested.

MAKING LIFE EASIER

Living with someone with an autistic disorder who has good language and skills is, on balance, more difficult than living with someone who is more severely disabled and obviously dependent on others. The more able older children and adolescents often want to be as independent as their age peers and are unwilling to accept parental authority. Some suggestions can be made to smooth the path a little for parents and teachers.

i *At home*

Most of the points made in this section are applicable at school as well as at home.

It is important to make the essential home or school rules very clear and to make sure the child understands that they are applicable to everyone. The children are resentful if they think they are being unfairly picked on, but are more likely to follow rules that are to be obeyed by everyone in the family or the class. Asperger wrote that his children were more willing to obey rules that were expressed as universally applicable rather than directed at them specifically. 'Everyone in this house, (school, family) must . . .'. The drawback is that, once stated in this way, the child with the autistic disorder will be the first to notice and object if someone else breaks the rule. They are less concerned about their own violations.

Never become angry or emotional. This is easy to say, difficult to do, but very helpful if you can. Remain cool, detached, judicious and absolutely fair to all. The children cannot cope with strong emotions, whether in themselves or other people. Faced with such emotion shown overtly, they tend to become distressed, angry and negative in reaction. Parents find particularly distressing the fact that the more able children do not respond to appeals to act or behave in particular ways in order to please or to spare the parents' feelings. The children cannot empathize because they have little or no capacity to understand other people's thoughts and feelings. Many parents have been deeply hurt by the apparent lack of feeling in their child. This is yet another reason why early diagnosis is so important. When parents are given a full explanation of the nature of autistic disorders, they find it much easier to accept the apparent callousness. They can then begin to develop the more objective non-emotional approach that works so much better.

Avoid head-on confrontation whenever possible. The children will always win an open battle because they have no inbuilt submission to authority or desire to please. Furthermore, punishment will not deter them. Negotiation and compromise are more helpful. If it is absolutely essential that they obey an edict, then the adult in charge has to be calmly implacable and indifferent to the child's techniques of opposition. It can take a very long time, so endless patience is required.

Avoid involvement in arguments. Some children are skilled at finding loopholes in every point you make and you cannot win. The same is true if they want to pursue questions on a particular topic. One way to terminate a discussion that is getting nowhere is to say, calmly but firmly, that the subject is now closed. Sometimes it is helpful to give a child a precise amount of time, perhaps five minutes, in which to ask questions or discuss and to stick rigidly to this.

Most children with autistic conditions, especially those who are more able, continually test the boundaries laid down by parents and teachers. Some appear deliberately to tease and defy. However, this trait also is not due to 'naughtiness' but follows from the lack of development of an internalized system of rules for social interaction. The testing behaviour is minimized in environments that are structured and organized, where the rules are fair and given in ways that are absolutely clear to the children and where the adult authority figures are all calm and consistent in their approach and all follow the same line. The aim is to help the children develop, over time, some internalized rules for living, even though these tend to be rigid and inflexible.

The children do not understand ambiguity or double meanings and take everything literally. They are confused by sarcasm or irony, which should be avoided when talking to the children.

The needs of brothers and sisters are important but can be overlooked by parents struggling to cope with a child with an autistic disorder. This subject is discussed in more detail in Chapter 15.

ii *At school*

The points made below are particularly relevant for children attending mainstream schools or other types of school that do not specialize in teaching children with autistic disorders. The advantages and disadvantages of different types of schooling are discussed in Chapter 18.

The children have no concept of hierarchy based on age, class, lines of authority or anything else – they are natural democrats. They say what they think with no regard for the consequences or other people's feelings. These attributes, which have their admirable side even if infuriating at times, are not due to rebelliousness or cheekiness. It helps to be aware of this and to avoid getting annoyed.

Despite their apparent self-assurance and indifference to authority, most more able children with autistic disorders have a very low self-esteem even if they are of high ability. They have all experienced many failures in social interaction and are sensitive to the laughter and scorn of their age peers when they behave in a naive way. Some develop a paranoid attitude as a result. These sensitivities should be borne in mind when teaching or caring for the children.

It helps to take every opportunity to involve the more able children in pursuits that raise their self-esteem, such as physical activities of the kind they are good at (if any), music, taking part in quizzes that need a good rote memory. Some (though not all) of the children have no fear and love performing in front of an audience. Finding them the right type of part in a school play or other special occasion and giving them enough coaching can be most rewarding for all concerned.

Most of the children like to be praised. However, there are a few who, paradoxically, become angry and negative if praised for anything, even though they have poor self-esteem. There is no known explanation for this, unless it is dislike of being picked out as different in any way. If a child has this trait, care has to be taken to avoid verbal commendation. Other, non-verbal, ways of showing approval should be tried.

The children often do not realize that, when the whole group is addressed, they are included. It is necessary to ensure that their attention is gained in class. When doing this, it is important to remember their sensitivity to being picked out unfairly, so gaining their attention has to be done tactfully.

It is important to find ways to use the children's positive skills in learning and not to concentrate on the things they cannot do. The desire to learn can often be encouraged by working with the child's special interests and linking teaching with these interests as far as possible. For example, if some ingenuity is used, a fascination with trains could be utilized in teaching art, physics, mathematics, English, geography, even history. If, however, there is a particular subject that a child refuses even to try to learn, it is best to compromise. The child can be allowed to pursue a personal interest quietly for that particular time as long as the rest of the class is not disturbed.

Various kinds of specific learning disorders are often associated with autistic conditions in more able children. These should be identified by psychological assessment so that they can be addressed in the teaching plan. Some of the children are much better at visuo-spatial skills than at understanding language, even if they have fluent speech. For such children, presenting concepts in visual rather than verbal terms is very helpful. Some, on the other hand, have specific visuo-spatial difficulties but have better expressive language, though they usually have problems with aspects of language comprehension. Teaching has to be adjusted to help them cope with these problems.

Poor physical coordination is common, though by no means universal. This may be present for most motor activities, even though the child has some special skill, such as playing a musical instrument or making constructional toys, that does require good coordination. For those with poor coordination in large movements, team games can be a nightmare. Efforts should be made to find some kind of physical activity that is within the child's capacity, so that they can hold their own with their age peers in at least one pursuit.

Break times and lunch hours in school are particularly stressful for the children because they are unstructured. Supervision is necessary to ensure that they do not become distressed, or engage in bizarre, stereotyped behaviour. They may cope better if allowed to stay inside working on a computer, or doing something else that they like. If they are outside with the other children they need to be protected from bullying and teasing. It may be necessary to explain to other children something of the problem

The Autistic Spectrum

and to call on their sympathy. The way to do this is to emphasize the child's special gifts as well as problems. This should always be done, if at all, in consultation and with the agreement of the parents.

Not all of the children have a bad time in mainstream schools or schools for a mix of disabilities. Some of the children have a special skill, such as playing a musical instrument, ability with maths and a willingness to help others with their homework, or dexterity with constructional kits, which may be admired by their classmates. Some who are quiet and gentle are befriended by another child and thereby enjoy a protector. It requires good supervision and observation to discover how any of the children with autistic disorders are coping, because of their inability to express their own feelings.

Adolescence

As with all children with autistic disorders, adolescence may bring a period of disturbed behaviour in some, though in others it can be the time when progress is accelerated. The problems that occur tend to be related to four particular concerns, namely desire for independence, increasing awareness of disability, wanting friendships and sexual relationships and pressures of exams at school.

DESIRE FOR INDEPENDENCE

Regardless of the level of ability, adolescence is associated with increasing size, strength and assertiveness. Those who are more able often want the same freedoms as their age peers, even though they are naive, immature and are not at all street-wise. Ideally, home and school should cooperate in teaching rules for sensible conduct so that some freedom can be allowed. This teaching has to begin early and be carried on for years. It helps, but no list of rules can ever be long enough to cover all possible situations that are met in real life. With the more able group, parents have to

accept some risks because they cannot keep a determined teenager under their supervision all the time. All they can do is to
make the rules of conduct outside the home as clear as possible
and to teach the young person where to turn for help in an
emergency.

The more able adolescents with autistic disorders, especially
those with the pattern described by Asperger, sometimes show
their growing assertiveness by blaming their parents for all their
troubles, despite all the love and care they have received through
their childhood. They may give trivial or bizarre reasons for their
hostility towards their parents. One teenager, for example, said
that all his difficulties were due to the fact that his parents would
not buy him an extremely expensive computer that he wanted
when he was eight years old. Such accusations can make parents
feel guilty even if they know they are irrational. The best way to
cope is for the parents to remain calm and to refuse to be drawn
into arguments and justifications of their actions. If the hostility
becomes intense and cannot be resolved, it may be best to seek
some form of accommodation away from home, such as a residential school (see Chapter 18).

A small minority of more able adolescents are so determined
to have their own way that they try to dominate the rest of the
family. In a few cases, the individual is so domineering that the
rest of the family have no life of their own. They have to fit in
with the often bizarre, repetitive pattern of life imposed upon
them to avoid temper tantrums and aggressive behaviour. In all
cases of this kind that I have met, the diagnosis of an autistic
disorder, usually Asperger's syndrome, has not been made in
childhood so the family is bewildered by the behaviour of the
individual concerned. When the diagnosis is made in early childhood, it is possible for the parents and teachers to provide the
necessary structured and organized environment and to lay down
and enforce sensible rules before adolescence begins. Once this
type of situation has developed, the only recourse for the parents
is to ask for help from the social services and from psychiatric
services through referral by the family doctor. Sorting out the
diagnosis is the first priority, before any action to relieve the
stress on the family can be initiated. It is important for the parents

to tell the whole story to the professionals involved. They should not try to hide the full extent of the difficulties in an effort to protect their disabled son or daughter, who is just as damaged by being allowed to dominate the home as are the rest of the family. In most cases, the only solution is some form of residential provision away from home (see Chapter 18).

Asperger noted, in his first paper, that individuals with his syndrome tend to be strongly attached to their own homes. The attachment is to the physical surroundings rather than to the family. This sometimes leads to intense dislike of leaving home even for an overnight stay somewhere and even more so for a longer holiday. It is paradoxical that a desire for personal independence can be combined with a refusal to leave the family home. When it is present in marked form, the attachment to home can make holidays a misery for the whole family. With teenagers or adults who can manage on their own for a few days, it may be best to leave them at home while the rest of the family have a break. This problem does not occur in everyone with Asperger's syndrome. Some love journeys and new places and are at their best on holidays when there is plenty to occupy them.

AWARENESS OF DISABILITY

It is difficult to know how far young children are aware of their disabilities. They certainly feel intense distress when they are frustrated or confused by their environment. The more able children are likely to have a fair amount of insight by the time they reach adolescence. They may express this in their own way. One boy used to say, very sadly, when he failed at some task, 'Can't do it. Got no brain.' A girl of 14 once asked her mother, 'Mummy, when God made me, why didn't he make me quite right?'. Some teenagers want to know why they are different from their siblings or their age peers. The response to developing insight varies, depending upon the personality and temperament of each individual. Some accept without becoming distressed, some become unhappy and depressed and some try to cope by denying that they have any problems and becoming angry if the subject is mentioned.

The young people who accept without concern are the most fortunate and easiest to live with. Those who react with distress need support from their family and others with whom they have close contact. Occasionally adolescents with autistic disorders who are concerned about themselves will do something inappropriate to overcome their problems. One young man suddenly decided he would improve his health if he took up running, so he promptly set out and ran for miles in bitterly cold weather in his vest and pants and was found in an exhausted condition a long way from home. It may not be possible to predict, and therefore prevent, this kind of impulsive behaviour. It is also impossible to shield more able adolescents from the knowledge that they do have particular problems that are not shared by most other people.

In order to improve their self-esteem, their positive skills should be emphasized and praised. It is often helpful to point out, as Asperger did, that there are many other people who are like them and that some are high achievers in art or science. Some ask if they have a 'mental illness'. It is reasonable, because sufficiently near the truth, to explain that the basic problem is not an illness but a different type of organization of the brain that has advantages as well as disadvantages. It can be pointed out that everyone is good at some things and less good at others. The more able person with autism is poor at understanding other people and expressing their own feelings, but is good in some other areas. It may help them to know that many people admire and envy the special skills that the person with an autistic disorder does have. An explanation of this kind can be tailored to suit each individual, taking into account their level of understanding. If possible, in the course of everyday life, their help should be elicited in situations in which their special skills can be put to good use.

It is difficult to help the adolescents who deny any disability even though it is obvious that, underneath, they are aware and unhappy. Any attempt at a discussion along the lines suggested above tends to provoke rage and further denial. The only course of action is to say nothing but to be prepared to give support if and when the individual shows the need.

Some more able adolescents are unconcerned that they have no friends and are not interested in having a girl or boy friend. Others realize that they have great difficulty in forming relationships and cope by deciding that they are not going to try. The majority are very aware of and distressed by their inability to form friendships, or to maintain them if they are ever started. Their capacity to comprehend the meaning and nature of friendship is often limited. They lack the instinctive knowledge of how to make the first moves prior to becoming accepted by others. If they do begin a relationship, they are often unable to give and take and may make inappropriate demands on the other person.

As in all other spheres of life, the adolescent with an autistic disorder has to be taught the basic rules of social interaction with age peers, which are not easy to formulate. Joining some clubs or groups can be a source of pleasure and help in developing social skills. This is likely to work best if the group caters for the interests of the individual concerned. Train spotters' clubs may attract those who are fascinated by trains. Chess clubs are excellent for the enthusiasts for this game. Social clubs that are not dedicated to some particular pursuit are less likely to be acceptable. Sometimes friendships do develop between group members with similar personalities and interests. In such cases, they tend to talk at each other on their particular subject, happily reeling off lists of train numbers or details of chess games without any true conversational interchange.

On the whole, the desire for a girl or boy friend is motivated more by the wish to copy what most other people of their age do rather than the need for an emotional relationship. Nevertheless, there is often a strong determination to succeed. Many of the young people have asked parents or teachers if there are books that will tell them how to get a partner and how to talk to them. To increase the difficulties, the boys often have very specific requirements for a girl friend, such as long blonde hair and blue eyes. The girls do not seem to be so choosy.

Establishing this sort of relationship is far harder than starting an ordinary friendship. Very often, if a teenage boy finds a girl friend, she terminates the relationship in a short time because she soon realizes how odd he is, how socially gauche and how little he is aware of her emotional or practical needs. For example, a 17-year-old boy with an autistic disorder made friends with a younger girl, whom he regarded as his special girl friend. His mother suggested that it would please the girl if he gave her a birthday present. 'All right,' said the boy, 'I will if she gives me the money'. He was very surprised when she ceased to have anything to do with him. Little can be done to help apart from teaching social skills as far as is possible, providing emotional support and pointing out that many people live satisfying lives without a sexual partner.

If there is a specific interest in the physical aspects of sex, teaching rules concerning appropriate behaviour in this area of life is particularly important and as much supervision as possible in the light of the individual's age and level of ability should also be organized. Indiscriminate displays of affection or naive encouragement of physical contact, such as touching and tickling, should be firmly discouraged where they are inappropriate. If for any reason a girl is particularly vulnerable and cannot be supervised all the time, advice on contraception should be sought.

PRESSURE OF EXAMS

Many of the most able adolescents with autistic disorders follow the national curriculum whether in mainstream or special schools. Some have no problems and do well academically. Others find the work at secondary level increasingly difficult. They kept up with the rest of the class, ostensibly at least, at the primary stage because they used their good rote memories. Secondary education requires adequate understanding of what is learnt and the ability to make connections and draw conclusions rather than just remembering. When preparations for exams begin, some of the pupils with autistic disorders experience high levels of stress. This causes some to give up and refuse to attend school. One teenager, for example, took to his bed and would not get up. Some struggle on without complaint but do badly in the exams. Others develop behaviour problems or a diagnosable psychiatric illness, usually depression (see below, under 'Adult life'), before or during the exams. Very few return to education after such an event.

Early diagnosis, accurate assessment of the child's level of ability and placement in the most appropriate type of school all help to avoid later problems due to exam pressures. When exams approach, sensitive supervision and careful observation by teachers and parents help to detect early signs of trouble. Special facilities for taking the exam, perhaps with a known supervisor and away from the large examination hall, may be sufficient. If the problems are too severe to solve in such ways, it is best to allow the young person to drop out altogether rather than risk a severe breakdown. If a breakdown of the kind to be described below does occur, then the exams cannot be taken.

Adult life

The major concerns for the more able adults with autistic disorders are living accommodation, employment and whether or not they can marry or live with a partner and start a family.

LIVING ACCOMMODATION

Taking the whole range of autistic disorders, including those with high levels of skill and no disabilities except for the triad of impairments in the most subtle form, it is possible to say with some confidence that the majority of the most able adults are able to live independently. That still leaves a large number who do not develop sufficient self-care, domestic and practical skills, or common sense, to have their own homes.

A proportion continue to live with their parents. This may

work fairly well if the individual concerned has regular sheltered or open employment, some leisure activities and is reasonably helpful and cooperative in the home. Some, however, have no outside activities of any kind because they have no paid work and there is no sheltered employment that is suitable in the local area. In such cases, the adult stays at home engaged in their repetitive activities, or watching the same videos, or doing nothing. The longer this goes on the less likely is the person concerned to want to lead a more active life. A small number may come to dominate the life of the family in the way described previously in this chapter. These situations arise because of the lack of day and residential services suitable for more able people with autistic disorders in many areas of the UK. Parents in this situation may find support and help from the National and their Local Autistic Society.

For the adults who are unable to work or live independently, the best solution is residential accommodation in a home specifically for more able people with autistic disorders. Most of these have been set up by the National or Local Autistic Societies (see Chapter 18). However, adults in this group can be found in every possible kind of sheltered accommodation, suitable or unsuitable. Some can be found among those living rough on the streets. Most who are unsuitably placed have never been diagnosed, so that it was never possible to make sensible plans for their future while they were still children.

EMPLOYMENT

Appropriate employment, whether open or sheltered, that makes use of special skills and is enjoyed is the best way to maximize self-esteem and minimize disturbed behaviour. More able adults with autistic disorders are employed in a wide range of paid occupations. In addition to level of ability and area of special skill, certain factors are important for success. A sympathetic and knowledgeable employer and tolerant workmates are among the essentials. The social and communication impairments exclude work that involves much interacting and talking with people. The autistic lack of flexibility means that work where instructions are complicated and methods change frequently is likely to be unsuitable. Some of the adults may still be sensitive to noises and bright lights and may be unable to tolerate such conditions in a workplace. They tend to be upset if people are impatient or irritable or if anyone shouts loudly. When they start work they need someone to explain every little detail, to show them the cloakroom and toilets, how to collect lunch from the canteen, what time to start work and, equally important, when to stop. Someone needs to keep a watchful eye to make sure everything goes smoothly. Even the journey to work may have unexpected snags. With public transport there is the risk that the usual bus or train may be late or cancelled and this may produce confusion and distress.

Those who can fit into open employment tend to be hard-working and conscientious. Once they have learned the rules they apply them with meticulous accuracy, although this can have its negative side, since striving for perfect accuracy may slow the work down to a level that is unacceptable. They are usually honest and without guile. If things go well, they are often popular with their colleagues, once their disabilities are understood and accepted. Problems arise when employers and workmates are not aware of the nature of the individual's specific impairments.

There are some among the more able adults who, despite their skills, are unable to cope with open employment, often because they are too rigid and repetitive to fit in with the demands of paid work. They require sheltered employment of the kind and in the conditions that are right for them. There are few specialized centres to cater for this group. Day centres for people with learning difficulties tend not to be able to provide for or to cope with those with autistic disorders, especially those who are more able, unless they have some staff with relevant training and experience and can make special provision.

The experimental scheme, run by the National Autistic Society, for helping more able adults to find and adapt to employment, is described in Chapter 18.

MARRIAGE

One of the questions often asked by parents of young children with autistic disorders is 'Will he/she ever marry and have children?'. To date, follow-up studies of people who have been diagnosed in childhood as having autistic disorders show that virtually none of them marry. This is to be expected, given the severe social impairments.

The adults who may marry are those who have the triad of impairments in the most subtle form, are of average or high ability and, in most cases, have never been diagnosed as having an autistic disorder. Such marriages can work well if the partner values the person with the autistic disorder for their positive qualities and knows and accepts their eccentricities. When things go wrong, this is often because the partner wants empathy and much emotional support, which the person with the autistic disorder cannot give.

Another source of difficulty is the autistic insistence on following a routine in the home that cannot be changed whatever the circumstances. Among the wives of men with autistic traits, there are some who seek help because of the stress of their everyday lives. In most cases they married without awareness of the problems ahead, or else thought that their influence would change their husbands. It is not possible to change anyone's character and behaviour pattern, least of all someone with autistic traits. After a varying length of time they realise this and do not know what to do. There are, in effect, only two courses of action. One is to accept the partner as they are and cope as well as possible; the other is to end the marriage or partnership. These are stark choices, especially if children are involved, but it is better to face the truth.

The advent of children may make things worse because their demands increase the need for mutual support between the parents. Furthermore, babies and toddlers tend to disrupt any attempts at an orderly life. As already mentioned (Chapter 7) there is good evidence for genetic factors in the cause of autistic disorders. The figures that are available to date concern the risk to parents of having a second child with an autistic disorder if they already have one. There are no statistics concerning the risks if one or both parents have an autistic disorder or have social or communication impairments or repetitive behaviour in a subtle form, but it seems likely that the risks are higher than for the general population.

Psychiatric illness

Psychiatric illnesses can complicate autistic disorders in adolescence or adult life. They are diagnosed mainly in those who are more able and can thus give some account of symptoms.

The condition that occurs most often is depression. This tends to be associated with the development of some insight and the recognition of difference from age peers. Lack of friends, especially girl or boy friends, or failures of attempts at such relationships are frequent causes of depression. In many, probably the majority, the symptoms are relatively mild and are reactive to specific problems. Sometimes, however, the depression is severe, affecting appetite, sleep and general level of activity. Psychiatric treatment, including anti-depressive medication, may be needed in such cases. Counselling from someone who understands and is experienced with people with autistic disorders can be most helpful for the more able adolescents and adults who are unhappy and finding it difficult to come to terms with their disabilities.

Other diagnosable psychiatric illnesses are less common. Episodes of mania or hypomania, or cycles of mania and depression can occur and require the appropriate treatment. The diagnosis of schizophrenia is particularly difficult to make in someone with an autistic disorder. The 'negative' symptoms, such as lack of social interaction, paucity of speech and non-verbal communication, and lack of motivation, are common in both conditions. The 'positive' symptoms of schizophrenia, that is the auditory hallucinations and delusional experiences, are difficult or impossible to describe for someone with the communication impairments of autistic disorders. Most people with autistic disorders, even those with good grammar and large vocabularies, have problems in understanding the meaning of questions to elicit the subjective experiences typical of schizophrenia. When confused and not knowing how to reply, they may say yes to anything. A young man who worked in an office became agitated when he had to use a different room at work while his own was being painted. He was so disturbed in behaviour that he was admitted to a psychiatric unit. He had never previously been diagnosed as having an autistic disorder. He was asked if he heard voices when no one was in the room with him, to which he replied that he had just had this experience. Schizophrenia was suspected until it was discovered that he was referring to the fact that he could overhear speakers in the next room through the thin partition. On taking a history from his parents, an autistic disorder of the Asperger type was diagnosed. Much care is needed before concluding that schizophrenia is present but, if such an illness does occur in someone with an autistic disorder, it should be treated appropriately, including giving the most effective medication.

This story illustrates another aspect of the psychiatric complications of autistic disorders. When under stress, even a previously able and comparatively well-adjusted adolescent or young adult can become disturbed in behaviour with rambling and incoherent speech. Actions can appear to be random and wildly inappropriate. The term 'psychotic' is often used for such states but adds nothing to one's understanding of them. They are not the same as schizophrenia though there may be non-specific delusions and hallucinations and odd perceptual experiences. The problems usually disappear if the source of stress can be identified and removed.

In a few adolescents or young adults, the repetitive routines of childhood develop into behaviour like that seen in obsessive-compulsive disorders. This may take the form of constant hand washing, or insistence on performing certain actions, such as doing up buttons in a precise way and starting again if any errors are made, or thinking the same thoughts repetitively. Phobias such as fear of germs can become intense and be accompanied by repetitive rituals to prevent contamination. This raises interesting questions concerning the relationship between autistic disorders and obsessive-compulsive states. The medication that has been found helpful in treating obsessive-compulsive states may be effective for this type of behaviour in people with autistic disorders.

A very small proportion of adolescents and young adults gradually become slower and slower in their actions. They may become fixed in postures, perhaps with a spoon of food halfway to their mouths and stay in this state for some seconds, minutes or even longer. They may have difficulty in crossing thresholds between rooms or demarcations between two types of flooring, taking tiny steps forward and then back, over and over again. They may be unable to initiate any action, such as rising from a chair, unless prompted by seeing someone else do this. They may cease speaking and lose all initiative, including not going to the toilet so that bladder and bowels fill to overflowing. This is called catatonia. It seems to be an inability to make an effort of will to initiate a movement. It is just like the catatonic states that followed the epidemic of encephalitis lethargica that occurred during and after the First World War and that were shown in the film of Oliver Sacks' book on the subject, called *Awakenings*. In some cases, this state is reached after the individual has gone through the stage of developing obsessive-compulsive behaviour. The repetitive rituals take longer and longer and the movements become slower and slower until finally the person is in a catatonic state.

In people in catatonic states, the automatic patterns of movement that were learnt before the catatonia started can still be carried on as long as the individual is helped to begin. Actions such as riding a bicycle, jumping on a trampoline or returning a football may be possible. Also, moving along a well-defined path is easier than crossing open unmarked ground. These facts give a guide for helping those affected. They must not be left to sit doing nothing but should be prompted through all the activities of each day. They should be encouraged to engage in all the automatic sequences of movement they developed prior to the catatonia. It should be noted that it may be as hard for the person concerned to stop such movements once started as it was to start them in the first place. The activities should be monitored so that they are not carried on to the point of exhaustion. It has been reported that anti-depressive medication has proved helpful in some cases of catatonia but the effects of medication are very variable and prescribing is a matter of trial and error.

Catatonia can occur in adolescents and young adults with autistic disorders of any level of ability. The reasons why it happens are not known, neither is there any work on what proportion of individuals are affected, although it is clear that the numbers are very small.

For all psychiatric illnesses that complicate autistic conditions, the appropriate treatment should be given but the underlying autistic disorder must not be overlooked. The special needs resulting from this long-term disability remain, even if the psychiatric complication is successfully treated. Ideally, adult as well as child psychiatrists should have training and experience with autistic disorders because they will meet people with these disabilities in all areas of their clinical work. They should be aware of the services they need so that they can refer them on to the relevant agencies for long-term help.

Delinquent and criminal behaviour

Adolescents and adults with autistic disorders who have mild learning difficulties or borderline, average or high levels of ability may commit acts that bring them into conflict with the law. This happens to only a small minority. The majority are extremely law-abiding because they are concerned to follow the rules in every tiny detail.

There are various reasons why a few break the law. Some are unaware that particular laws apply to them and cannot understand what all the fuss is about. One young man took money from his aunt's house because he thought it would buy him some friends. He found it in a drawer, not her handbag, so innocently assumed he could take it.

The pursuit of special interests can lead to trouble. An adolescent girl was fascinated by the characteristics of different breeds of dogs, though she had no liking for real dogs. She took some books on dogs from a bookshop without paying. She did this twice without being detected but, on the third occasion, she was caught. She was indignant because she thought that the fact that no-one stopped her on the first two occasions demonstrated that she was allowed to take the books she wanted. Her evident oddness and guileless innocence saved her from prosecution.

In a small number of cases, the social impairment takes the form of total indifference to other people. If this is allied to a special interest in, for example, weapons or chemicals, there may be the temptation to try the effects on someone.

Paranoid feelings may be particularly strong in a few individuals, often based on real experiences of rejection or teasing by age peers. The desire for revenge can lead to physical aggression, attacks on property, or some other illegal act. Parents may be the object of such attacks if they are undeservedly blamed for the individual's problems.

Occasionally, a teenage boy attaches himself to a group of age peers who engage in delinquency. The young person with the autistic disorder follows the gang because it is the nearest approach to friendship he can find. It is likely that, sooner or later, he will be the one member of the gang who is caught while the others are quick enough to run away.

As already emphasized, the proportion who carry out delinquent or criminal acts is very small. If the diagnosis is made in early childhood and appropriate education and a structured, organized programme are provided, the chances of illegal behaviour occurring in adolescence or adult life are minimized. If such problems do occur, or seem likely, parents should seek help from psychiatric and social services and the Local or National Autistic Society. As mentioned before, it is of no help to anyone, least of all to the young person with an autistic disorder, to try to hide the problems.

The borderlines with normality

Many of the features that are characteristic of autistic disorders can be found in lesser form in individuals who are functioning well in all aspects of life. Most people can identify one or more aspects of their own personalities that have something in common with autistic behaviour. As Asperger pointed out, some degree of autism is an advantage for those in the fields of art or science.

There is no clear cut-off point between autistic disorders in the most able people and what might be called eccentric normality. In discussions on problems of diagnosis it is often asked where the line should be drawn. Is there not a danger of harming someone by giving them a diagnosis and causing problems that did not exist before? This is a theoretical rather than a practical dilemma. In clinical work, the primary reason for making a diagnosis of an autistic disorder is that the individuals concerned are experiencing major difficulties in development from infancy to adult life and their parents, or occasionally the persons themselves, are asking for help. In these circumstances it is appropriate to investigate in order to make a diagnosis from which recommendations can follow. Individuals who are coping well, even if they have many autistic traits, will not be referred, or refer themselves, for diagnosis and it would be an unwarranted interference to suggest that they should. A group of very able people who are aware that they have an autistic disorder and who keep in touch with each other have made the point in various publications that their way of thinking and experiencing the world is valid for them and they would not want to be 'cured' even if this were possible. By no means all those with insight feel this way and some do ask for help even though they are, ostensibly, coping well. The feelings and wishes of each individual should be respected.

Sisters and brothers

Some studies of the effects on children of living with a sibling with various kinds of disabilities, including autistic disorders, have been described and have given conflicting results. It seems that some children are adversely affected whereas others cope well. The effects are related to a whole series of definable and indefinable factors, including the severity of the disability, whether or not the child has disturbed behaviour, the personalities of the brothers and sisters and the attitudes of the parents.

Those with siblings with autistic disorders do face a number of special problems. Perhaps the hardest thing for them is that their parents have to give so much time and attention to the special child that there is little to spare for the rest of the family. This is particularly likely to affect a sister or brother who is close in age to the child with the disability. Parents need to be aware of this danger and do their best to set aside time for their other children and to show them that they are equally loved and valued. If it is possible to arrange for some domestic help, this may enable the parents to organize their time more easily.

A destructive child may break toys and other things. Brothers and sisters need to have a special safe place to lock away their precious possessions and, if possible, a room of their own. Parents should, if possible, replace damaged possessions and should try to teach children with autistic disorders not to touch any objects except their own. If sisters and brothers are reassured that their rights are being respected, they are likely to accept the occasional loss of a possession with better grace.

Siblings of school age may feel unable to bring their friends home to play. If at all possible, parents should encourage friends to visit. It is best to explain about autism frankly and simply and to answer the questions of the brothers and sisters and their friends in as calm and relaxed a manner as possible. The child with the autistic disorder may be able to play with the others but, if they habitually disrupt activities, parents should try to arrange for their other children and friends to have at least some time to themselves.

Many children enjoy playing with and teaching their sibling with an autistic disorder and can involve them in a variety of activities. Brothers and sisters are often more successful in this than their parents. Children with a sibling who is disabled in any way often develop a level of maturity beyond their years and many go into the caring professions in adult life. Parents of children with autistic disorders have to beware of placing too much responsibility on the shoulders of their other children and to make sure that they have plenty of time for their own pursuits. Parents are naturally concerned about the future of their child who is disabled and some may hope that a sister or brother will eventually take on the responsibility of care. This is a hard burden to place on young shoulders and could, if taken seriously by the sibling, disadvantage them throughout their lives. It is best to let brothers and sisters make their own decisions as to how much involvement they can sustain rather than subjecting them to emotional pressure, overt or covert.

There are some brothers or sisters who find it hard to interact with a child with an autistic disorder. Their feelings should be respected and they should not be pressurized to be involved or made to feel guilty. This can be hard advice for a parent who is desperate for help but a reluctant, resentful helper is worse than no helper at all.

The siblings, before they understand the nature of autism, may worry about the possibility of themselves developing autistic behaviour. They may have all kinds of alarming fears and fantasies and parents need to be sensitive to these feelings. They can help by their calm acceptance of all their children, their willingness to discuss and to explain and their love and reassurance.

Adolescents are often concerned about the possibility of their own future children having autistic disorders. As discussed in Chapter 7, there is an increased risk of another child with an autistic disorder, or with more subtle autistic traits, being born to parents who already have one child with typical autism. The precise risk of siblings having a child with the same type of disability has not been calculated but it seems likely that it is higher than that for the general population. The exact risk must vary depending on the cause in the affected child. For example, if it is known that the cause was rubella in the mother's pregnancy, genetic factors are much less likely. It puts the matter into perspective to explain that there are many different genetic and other conditions in addition to autistic disorders that can produce congenital disabilities and few families have no such problems in their past histories.

The journal of the National Autistic Society, entitled *Communication*, publishes occasional articles by sisters and brothers of children or adults with autistic disorders. Some find it helpful to meet or correspond with others in the same situation and can make contacts through the Society. Siblings are welcome at Local and National Society meetings.

·16·

Problems faced by parents

Parents have to cope with a series of problems, some of which are practical and some of which are emotional. Many of these are common to parents of children with any kind of disability, while others are special to the families of children with autistic disorders.

The parents of any child with a long-term disability have to undergo a change of attitude when they first learn the truth and this is a painful process. Like all parents, they start off with the expectation that they have a perfect baby who will grow up to be a fully independent adult. They have to adjust to the fact that all their hopes and plans for their child's future, and their own future as well, will have to be changed. They may have feelings of guilt, which are a waste of mental energy that can be turned to better use. Professional workers can help parents to develop a constructive attitude. The workers who fail to diagnose an autistic disorder and attribute the strange behaviour to parental mishandling, or recognize autism but consider that it is caused by the parents, do great harm to the families and the children. Such ideas are gradually becoming less common but still exist.

Autistic disorders in a child cause some special emotional problems for parents. The disability is not detectable at birth and is rarely diagnosed before 18 months at the earliest. Parents go through emotional swings, at times knowing that something is wrong and at other times persuading themselves that all is well.

They reassure themselves because the child's physical development gives no cause for alarm and, every now and again, the child does something so skilfully that it seems they must be highly intelligent. On the other hand, social aloofness, when it is present, is painful and baffling for the parents. It is a common experience for parents to feel that there must be one simple key, which, if found, could solve all the problems. Eventually the anxiety is seen to be justified and a professional opinion is sought. By this time the parents have swung so often between hope and despair that they may find the truth hard to accept.

Before the diagnosis is made, parents often feel they are the only people in the world to have a child with such strange behaviour and the knowledge that there are many others comes as a great relief. Meeting other parents through the Local Autistic Society is a source of emotional and practical support. The experience of emotional isolation in the child's early years is becoming less common as knowledge of autistic disorders increases but it still occurs. This is one of the major reasons for the importance of early and accurate diagnosis. Research into ways of identifying the basic impairments early in life is ongoing and making progress.

In the early years of a child with an autistic disorder, the parents' attachment makes them persevere, even if the child shows little or no response. Despite all the difficulties, the very weakness and dependence of a child with a disability tends to make the natural attachment of parent to child even stronger. This attachment has positive results in that the child is loved and cared for. The negative side is the tendency to give less attention to the other members of the family who are more independent but still need their parents' love and support. When progress does occur, each small step forward is the more rewarding because it was so long in coming.

Helping a child with an autistic disorder to develop skills and enjoy activities is hard work and time-consuming. Combining this with bringing up other children as well sounds like an impossible feat. The only solution is to organize a routine so that each member of the family has their fair share of the parents' attention. A short session with a parent regularly each day is better than longer sessions occurring sporadically. Parents should not forget themselves in their timetable. They need some rest and relaxation away from the family in order to preserve their sense of proportion. If their horizons are limited exclusively to the daily life of the child who is disabled, no one benefits, least of all the child concerned.

Children with autistic disorders can cause parents extra expense if they are destructive of clothing, furniture, windows, wallpaper and so forth. If they are not toilet trained, nappies have to be provided and sheets and other bedding continually washed. Parents should apply for the statutory financial benefits to which they are legally entitled.

The social life of the family tends to be restricted by a child with a disability, especially an autistic disorder. If they are disturbed in behaviour it may be difficult to find a baby-sitter so the parents may never be able to go out together. The Local Autistic Society may have a scheme for baby-sitting. If not, then the idea can be suggested and explored by interested members. Such schemes are always the result of individual initiatives.

Taking the child out in public can lead to problems. Most of them show no evidence of disability in their appearance. If they behave oddly, some strangers are critical and assume the child is 'spoilt'. A sensitive parent may avoid taking out the child, even on expeditions they might enjoy. For the sake of the child and the whole family, parents have to develop thick skins and take the child out as much as possible, ignoring the stares of the ill-educated. Teaching appropriate behaviour in public, beginning as early as possible, does help to reduce the major problems (see Chapter 10). Public awareness of and sympathy for people with autistic disorders has greatly increased since the first edition of this book was written, helped by publicity in all the media and the *Rain Man* film.

Most parents are concerned about having another child, especially if the one with an autistic disorder is their first. There is now strong evidence that there is a raised risk of parents having more than one child with an autistic disorder unless the cause in the first child is known and is clearly not genetic. The details have been given in Chapter 7. There are sources of genetic counselling and information on these can be obtained from the National Autistic Society. However, in the end, parents have to consider the facts as they relate to themselves and their families and make their own decisions.

The problems of other children in the family who themselves are developing normally are discussed in Chapter 15. These add to the parents' concerns. If siblings ask questions about autistic disorders, including the risk to themselves of having a child who is also affected, the best strategy is for parents to answer the questions with honesty when they are asked. If they are unsure of any facts, the National Autistic Society can recommend reading matter and suggest sources of expert advice.

Relatives often provide help and support. Grandparents, for example, can be a major source of emotional and practical help, including baby-sitting. Loving grandparents may develop a special relationship with the child, somehow finding a way round the social and communication impairments.

Unhappily, the attitudes of some relatives may be less constructive. They may feel that a child with a disability reflects badly on the whole family, thus disregarding the fact that all families have relatives with disabilities somewhere in their histories. They may try to lay the blame on one or other parent or their ancestry. They may reject the child and try to avoid seeing them or involving them in family affairs, visits or outings. Equally distressing is the relative who insists that there is nothing wrong with the child and that all the problems are due to the parents' methods of child-rearing and dealing with difficult behaviour. The best way to cope is to keep cool, calm and dignified, provide information but refuse to be drawn into arguments and, if there is no other way of changing attitudes, to see as little as possible of those who are unsympathetic.

It cannot be emphasized too strongly that autistic children vary very widely in the severity of their disabilities and in the amount of progress they can make, ranging from very little all the way to the achievement of independence in adult life. The parents of the children with the most severe disabilities have to cope with the sadness of seeing little improvement in their own child, while knowing others with autistic disorders who have made great strides. When the diagnosis is first made, all parents hope that their own child will be one of those with a good prognosis but follow-up studies have shown that a substantial number are not in this category. This is just one more hard fact among many with which parents of these children have to come to terms. It is pointless for them to waste time in blaming themselves for their child's problems. The constructive approach is to aim to find a way of life for each child in which they will be as happy and contented as possible, whatever their level of function. Parents whose children make good progress should avoid taking a superior attitude to others whose children do less well. When the children grow up, the parents of those who are more able often have to watch without being able to help while their sons or daughters try to become independent and suffer in the process. The parents of those with more severe disabilities who will be dependent on others all their lives are at least saved this source of distress.

Parents with children who will never become independent as adults worry about what will happen to their child when they themselves can no longer care for them. As already mentioned in Chapter 15, it is a great burden for siblings if parents apply emotional pressure to them to make them feel they should take over the future care of the child. The practical steps parents can take are to ensure that the child is known to the local social services, to investigate different types of residential accommodation well before this becomes essential and to obtain legal advice concerning wills and trusts if this is appropriate to the family's financial situation.

Unity within the family is a major factor in coping successfully with the strain of raising a child with an autistic disorder. It is important to avoid the temptation to blame the other partner for the child's behaviour. It does no good, and a lot of harm, to criticize each other for mishandling the child. Discussions concerning genetic traits in the family are interesting if pursued in the spirit of intellectual enquiry but not if they are used as the focus of blame. A series of sleepless nights and terrible days can try the patience of a saint but the effort of remaining calm and reasonable is well worthwhile. Keeping one's temper and refusing to nag or become irritable all become easier if worked at consistently. Good family relations have a beneficial effect on the child's behaviour, partly because any child is happier and easier to manage within a united family and partly because the proper handling of difficult behaviour demands a consistent approach from both parents, who must back each other's decisions in front of the child and reserve questions and discussions on methods for when they are alone together. Some parents are drawn closer together by the experience of having a child with a disability, while others are torn apart by the stress. Support from relatives on both sides of the family, help from professional workers and appropriate placements in pre-school units, schools and adult services all contribute to lessening the burdens on families. A sense of humour is also a great help. Many of the things that the children do and say are extremely funny, even if trying at the time they happen, and it does one good to laugh at them in retrospect.

Occasionally parents are faced with the dilemma of knowing another family with a child who they feel sure has an autistic disorder but whose parents are unaware or unwilling to face the possibility. If the child's parents do not know about autism, tactful enquiries and comments may prove to be the catalyst needed for the family to begin to find help. If on the other hand, the parents do not want to know, there is nothing to be done except to wait until they begin to acknowledge they are concerned and to be ready with help at the right moment.

·17·

The roles of professional workers

In this chapter the roles of different kinds of professionals in relation to autistic disorders will be discussed. The services within which the professionals work will be outlined in Chapter 18.

How well or how badly a visit to any professional worker goes depends on the child or adult concerned but also on the knowledge, experience and attitude of the professional involved and their assistants and receptionists. Parents or other carers should explain as much as they can and suggest ways of approaching the person with an autistic disorder. Most professionals are interested and willing to help. If a parent is unfortunate enough to meet one of the minority who are impatient or hostile, I would suggest that, afterwards, they should write a letter to the appropriate person, couched in positive terms, explaining about autism and suggesting how things could be managed better in future. It might be helpful if this was accompanied by a letter and some general information from the Local Autistic Society, perhaps inviting the professional and co-workers to the next open meeting. No opportunity for education should be lost.

Family doctors

Despite the increase in general awareness of autistic disorders many parents still have problems in finding out what is wrong with their child. Recognizing autistic disorders requires knowledge and experience but, because they are comparatively uncommon compared with many physical illnesses, most family doctors see only a few children and adults with these conditions. Doctors in general practice are much more familiar with physical symptoms and signs than with unusual behaviour in a child who looks alert, attractive and physically healthy. Even for professionals with experience, it is necessary to be cautious when diagnosing children under five years of age because major changes can occur later, particularly around five to six years.

The family doctor is often the first person to be approached by parents when they are concerned that something is wrong. Even though most family doctors cannot be experts in recognizing autistic disorders, they can listen to the parents, appreciate their concern and refer on to someone with specialist knowledge in the field of developmental disorders. They should avoid all of the three most unhelpful statements that can be made to a mother who is worried about her child's development. These are 'You are an over-anxious mother', 'He/she will grow out of it' and 'It must be the way you are bringing her/him up'.

TREATMENT OF PHYSICAL ILLNESSES AND DISABILITIES

A child with an autistic disorder may have any other type of physical disability or illness. The more disabilities a child has, the harder they find it to cope with life. It is therefore important to make sure that a child with an autistic disorder is as physically fit as possible and to give whatever remedial treatment is necessary. Diagnosis of any illness can be difficult because the children often do not complain and cannot describe their symptoms. Information from parents who know their child better than anyone else gives the best clues as to what is wrong.

Routine physical care, such as inoculations and treatment for physical illnesses, can be a problem because many of the children have intense resistance to interference. They dislike the change in routine, hate being touched and are disturbed by the unfamiliar smells, sights and sounds. However, it is surprising that some children and adults with autistic disorders actually like having medical attention. Some are indifferent to pain and are fascinated by the technical details of the procedures. Others seem to enjoy being the centre of so much attention and sympathy without having to do anything. With all children with disabilities, family doctors can do their work more effectively if they get to know the child and obtain their trust before they need any medical care.

Having to wait a long time to be seen is a strain for any child and particularly for those with autistic disorders who have no idea of the reason why they are in a strange place for so long. It is also hard on the parents and the other patients if the child's behaviour becomes disturbed. The understanding doctor should try to arrange appointments to avoid this problem, if the circumstances make this possible.

Paediatricians and psychiatrists

DIAGNOSIS AND MEDICAL INVESTIGATIONS

In the first edition of this book, there was the implicit assumption that diagnosis of autistic disorders was always made by a doctor. Now, a number of clinical psychologists have made these disorders their special field and have developed expertise in diagnostic methods. However, medically qualified professionals, especially paediatricians and child psychiatrists, are still numerically the most likely people to be required to diagnose developmental disorders. Their knowledge is needed for medical investigations and the recognition of any associated physical conditions.

Another problem over the last three decades has been the influence of the school of thought that denies the reality of mental illness and disability and is opposed to 'labelling'. Those who hold these views believe that giving a name to a condition is a self-fulfilling prophesy and harms the person concerned. In reality, having an accurate and detailed diagnosis as early as possible is the first crucial step for the parents, enabling them to find information and help and giving access to services and the support found from meeting other parents in the same situation. Although it is intensely distressing to know that their child has a serious developmental disability, most parents are relieved to have an explanation of the puzzling behaviour and the possibility of following a plan of action. In response to the anti-labelling theory, one parent pointed out that children with odd behaviour cannot avoid labels of some kind; she would rather have her child correctly diagnosed as autistic than labelled 'that spoilt child with awful behaviour'.

A full diagnostic evaluation involves taking a detailed developmental history, psychological assessment, observation of behaviour, examination for any additional medical or psychiatric conditions and disabilities, including impairments of hearing or vision and investigations to try to establish the original cause. With regard to the last, there are some differences of opinion. In Sweden, for example, a full medical work-up is carried out for all children referred to clinics for developmental disorders, including tests of blood and cerebro-spinal fluid. These ensure that no associated conditions are missed; they are informative for the parents and are of value for research. In the UK, the investigations are much less extensive unless there are clear clinical indications that particular tests should be done. This is because detailed investigations rarely show abnormalities that are relevant for treatment; they can be distressing for the child and they are expensive.

DISCUSSION WITH PARENTS

Many parents, by the time the diagnosis of an autistic spectrum disorder has been made, have already thought about the possibility – some have made their own diagnosis and just want confirmation. In this situation, they want the facts given in a sensitive but open and honest way. Even if they are not surprised by the diagnosis, they may have over-estimated their child's level of ability, so sympathy and understanding are needed in discussing this point. The long term prognosis for independence in adult life, including marriage and children, is another area of great concern. Not everyone wants to know about this when their child is young, so answering questions as they arise is often the best way to cope with these emotional issues. Plenty of time is needed to feed back to the parents the details of the medical and psychological findings and to answer all their questions. Ideally, more than one session should be available to talk over the implications of the diagnosis, but this is rarely possible in a clinic situation.

With progress in research on methods of early detection, it is possible that, in the future, the presence of an autistic disorder may be suspected in young children before the parents have become concerned. This already sometimes happens in paediatric practice. It is here that the most gentle and sensitive approach is required, tailored to the needs of the particular family. Even more difficult is the situation in which the parents know that their child has a developmental problem but refuse to accept the diagnosis of an autistic disorder. There is no general answer to such problems. Each situation has to be dealt with as seems best – for some, there is no good solution.

It is a hard task for a professional worker to have to tell parents that they have a child with a serious developmental disorder with implications for the long-term future. Professionals in this situation have to deal with their own emotions as well as those of the parents and it requires all their skill, experience and human compassion to handle the situation successfully.

TREATMENT FOR PSYCHIATRIC DISORDERS

Psychiatrists for adult psychiatric conditions or for learning difficulties may be called upon to treat adults with psychiatric illnesses associated with autistic disorders. The problems psychiatrists experience in recognizing autistic disorders, whether or not they are complicated by psychiatric illness, are discussed in Chapter 6.

PRESCRIBING MEDICATION

Medication may be used for sleep problems, calming disturbed behaviour or high anxiety, for self-injury, epileptic fits, or for psychiatric conditions complicating autistic disorders. The problems and limitations of drugs used for people with autistic disorders are noted in Chapter 10.

Dentists

Teeth cleaning can be a major problem in children with autistic disorders. They may be unable or unwilling to clean their own teeth and resist when their parents try. They may eat only soft or sweet foods and demand large quantities of drinks that are bad for the teeth. Gum disease, dental decay, toothache and even a dental abscess can occur without any sign from the child that something is wrong. Sometimes, the child's behaviour becomes disturbed in response to a painful condition, but they are unable to indicate the site of the problem.

Regular dental care is essential but may be hard to organize if the child refuses to cooperate. There are a number of dentists who have special experience because they have worked with disabled people in the school dental service, hospitals or community homes. They have developed excellent techniques for gaining the trust and cooperation even of children with severe autistic disorders. It often takes a long time before any treatment can be given but time taken to get to know the child is well spent. Some children, after intense resistance, change to enjoying their visits to the dentist. This is one of the many paradoxes presented by children with autistic disorders.

Clinical psychologists

ASSESSMENT

As already noted, some psychologists are involved in diagnosing the presence of autistic spectrum disorders. Their other specific role in the diagnostic process is assessment of the individual's pattern of abilities and disabilities. Standardized psychological tests of many kinds, together with observation of the child's behaviour in structured and unstructured situations, are used in this process. When the information obtained in this way is put together with the details of the developmental history, the behaviour in different settings and the medical findings, a complete diagnostic formulation can be made. This is of value for helping parents to understand their child and as a basis for planning education.

BEHAVIOUR MANAGEMENT

Psychologists have made a major contribution to helping children and adults with autistic disorders by developing methods of behaviour management through organization of the environment. Much has been learnt over the years of working in the field. Some of the original ideas have had to be modified or discarded but the environmental/behavioural approach to behaviour problems is still the most effective one that is currently available.

COUNSELLING

Some psychologists are engaged in individual or family counselling. This is discussed below.

Social workers

Social workers include those who are employed by the statutory social services, or by voluntary or other bodies, or who work privately. They have two kinds of roles. One is helping families to obtain all kinds of services and benefits that they need and to which they are entitled and the other is counselling individuals and families. Changes over recent years in legislation on the organization of the statutory social services combined with constraints on their budgets have greatly reduced the time available for individual and family counselling work. Social workers employed by other agencies or working privately still give this kind of help but those who are experienced with autistic disorders are few and far between.

One of the roles of social workers in the social services is to support families in their dealings with education, health and other statutory, voluntary and private bodies and they should coordinate the work of these agencies. This is a time-consuming, sometimes frustrating but highly important aspect of their work.

Educational psychologists

Research and practical experience has shown that the right kind of education is crucial for the development to their full potential of children with autistic disorders. Educational psychologists are concerned with assessment of children who are having learning difficulties at school, when requested by the school staff. Their role also includes advising teachers on special educational programmes for such children. With other professionals they are involved in the process of deciding if a child needs a formal Statement of Educational Needs and providing the appropriate reports if a Statement is to be made. In order for a child to have special educational help, their needs have to be formally recognized. The process of assessment of needs and making a formal 'Statement of Special Educational Needs' is outlined in Chapter 18.

Teachers

Teachers have the task of putting all the recommendations into effect in the classroom. They also have to work closely together with parents and other professionals involved. They need training, experience and sympathetic understanding of the children. Together with parents, carers in residential establishments and teachers have the most demanding roles of any who are involved with people with autistic disorders.

In mainstream schools, one or more teachers have the special role of Special Educational Needs (SEN) coordinators.

Speech and language therapists

Language problems are extremely common in autistic disorders but the fundamental impairments affect the way language is used for communication and not just the structure of language. The therapists who are interested in enhancing social and communication skills, including comprehension and use of all methods of communicating, have a valuable contribution to make. They may be the first to suspect that a child with a language problem has an autistic disorder and can contribute to the diagnostic assessment. In schools they can work directly with the children and guide teachers and parents in ways of enhancing the children's social and communication skills.

The language therapists who are of most help are those who are concerned with a child's whole pattern of behaviour and not solely with language. Too narrow a view of language therapy, ignoring the rest of the child's behaviour, can lead to the assumption that the language problem exists in isolation and to the denial of any underlying autistic disorder.

Other therapists

Various other professional workers can be involved in programmes for people with autistic disorders. They are included together under this heading because the roles overlap to some extent.

Physiotherapy and a programme of physical exercises can be helpful for the problems of motor co-ordination that are so common, especially organizing movements in relation to other people.

The skills of occupational therapists are valuable in devising and teaching constructive activities. They also may be involved with a range of physical activities.

Some music therapists are very interested in working with children or adults with autistic disorders because many of them are more responsive to music than to speech.

Aromatherapy, massage and techniques for encouraging relaxation, dance and drama are much enjoyed by many people with autistic disorders of all ages and may help to reduce tension and disturbed behaviour. Some people with the relevant skills have found it rewarding to work with children and adults with autistic disorders.

Teachers and instructors who can engage the children or adults in physical education and other physical pursuits of all kinds, including horse-riding and swimming, are much needed because of the positive effects of these activities.

The professional workers with these kinds of specialist training can all make a valuable contribution as members of a team involved with people with autistic disorders. Difficulties arise if workers in any one discipline assume that they alone can help or even cure these conditions. Another misconception that sometimes arises is that the specific disability being treated by the therapist is the cause of the whole clinical picture. One example, mentioned earlier, is that of 'semantic-pragmatic language disorder', which has been used as a diagnostic category, preventing recognition of an autistic disorder in more able children with fluent speech (see Chapter 6). Another is the theory that lack of integration of different kinds of sensory input is the basis of autistic behaviour, or even a separate diagnostic category. These ideas arise when the workers concerned do not take account of the whole history and clinical picture.

Counsellors

People whose original training is in psychology, psychiatry, social work or other professions may be involved in counselling either individuals with autistic disorders or parents and families, or both.

Sometimes adolescents and adults with autistic disorders who have made good progress and who are able to talk fairly well become unhappily aware that they are different from others of their age. Such a person may be helped by sensible and sensitive counselling from a psychologist or other professional worker who understands the nature of the disabilities. Individuals with autistic disorders can become depressed by the loss of someone they love and depend upon and by other major crises of life and may need the help of an experienced counsellor at these times. Some of those with good abilities who are trying to live independently rely upon ready access to practical advice and emotional support from a counsellor they like and trust.

For the parents, in the absence of any alternative, the main source of support, apart from their own family, is other parents in the same situation. Some families find they can accept a disabled child fairly easily and come to terms with their unhappiness as time goes on. Others are less philosophical, for a variety of personal reasons. Many would be helped by counselling from an experienced professional worker who understands what it is like to have a child with a developmental disability. Such counselling can help to diminish any tendency to self-blame and to release the parents' energies for more constructive activities in relation to their child. The times when support from an experienced counsellor are particularly needed are when the diagnosis of an autistic disorder is first made, when approaching school age and on starting school, when the child reaches adolescence, at school-leaving and at the time of admission to long-term residential care, whenever this may be.

Practical counselling, based on understanding of the nature of autistic disorders and solid common sense, is different from psychotherapy and psychoanalysis based on theoretical concepts of the human psyche. These latter two methods have been attempted with children and adults with autistic disorders, but there is no evidence that they are effective in curing or even diminishing the children's disabilities. The psychotherapeutic techniques that presuppose the development of complex language and the ability to introspect and understand symbolic ideas are particularly inappropriate. The interpretations given by the therapist are liable to confuse individuals with autistic disorders and to implant bizarre ideas, which they talk about on the most unsuitable occasions. Play therapy is equally pointless in children with impairments of imaginative development.

Professional workers who hold theories implying that the parents cause their child to become autistic may recommend that these parents should have psychotherapy or psychoanalysis, in order to help the child indirectly. There is no evidence that these methods are useful in practice. In so far as they exacerbate self-blame, they do harm.

Staff in day centres

Staff who work in day centres have a variety of past experience and training. Some are specialists in a particular skill or trade such as woodwork or metalwork. Specific training in working with adults with autistic disorders would be helpful but most have to learn through experience.

Residential care staff

Care workers in residential homes for adults also enter this work from many different backgrounds, including social work, psychiatric nursing and teaching. Many junior staff begin with no training. Courses and qualifications in general aspects of residential care work are available but, in the past, there has been little emphasis on the needs of adults with autistic disorders. Now, a training work book has been published, called *Autism Focus*, by Tom McKernon and John Mortlock.

Advocates of 'curative treatments'

Every condition that produces life-long disabilities and for which there is no effective treatment has been the focus of claims for curative methods. Autistic disorders are no exception. The so-called cures have included medications, diets, psychotherapies, behaviour therapies and methods that can only be described as mystical or magical. Some methods have come and gone only to return under another name or in another form. It must be emphasized that educational methods that have proved their worth in practice do not cure children of their autistic disorders. They facilitate the development of any potential skills. There is a close analogy with education for children with visual or hearing impairments. Education teaches them skills but does not cure their biological disabilities.

There are three main problems in evaluating any possible claims that a treatment is curative. First, almost all methods, except the most bizarre, tend to have a grain of truth in them. For example, holding and cuddling a child through a temper tantrum is helpful and holding accustoms the child to being held, but this does not mean that the basic impairments have been cured; teaching practical skills by guiding a child's limbs is a useful technique, but not a justification for the claims made for 'facilitated communication'; 'auditory integration therapy' may reduce oversensitivity to sound, but there is no objective evidence that it does anything else. Second, children with autistic disorders go through phases of more and less difficult behaviour and tend to develop skills in sudden spurts. If a good phase or acquiring a new skill coincides by chance with a new 'treatment' this could be credited with the improvement. Third, the outcome in adult life is closely linked to the innate level of ability. Those with high levels of skill are likely to do well as long as they are educated appropriately, whatever 'treatment' they receive. A therapist who selects the most able children for their special treatment is bound to have apparent successes.

Proper evaluation requires carefully organized and controlled trials by objective observers who are not involved in any way with the advocates of the treatments. There must be adequate methods of measurement of any changes and long-term follow-up of any later consequences of the method being assessed. The few methods that have been properly tested have been shown not to have the effects claimed.

Parents do, of course, have the right to try any treatment that is not potentially harmful and is ethically acceptable. They should, however, beware of those who play on parents' feelings of guilt and despair and the desire to clutch at any straw. The National Autistic Society publishes a booklet giving objective information concerning various 'treatments' that are available to date but does not advocate any of them.

·18·

Services for children and adults

In the past, most services for people with disabilities were provided directly by the National Health Service and the local authority social services and education authorities. Major changes have occurred over the years and now voluntary bodies and private agencies supply many of the direct services with the statutory authorities acting as purchasers. Evolution is still continuing so it is possible to give here only a brief outline of the services as they are at present. The aim is to give parents some idea of where to begin looking to find the help they need for their child.

Diagnosis and assessment

The diagnosis of an autistic disorder may be suspected first by the parents or by a variety of professionals in touch with the child such as health visitors, teachers, speech therapists. In the case of adults who have never been diagnosed in childhood, a psychiatrist for adult illnesses, a social worker or a residential care worker may be the first to suspect an autistic condition. For children, the first referral to confirm the diagnosis, made through the family doctor, is usually to the local paediatrician, child psychiatric or child guidance clinic. Parents may find all the information and help they need through these local resources. If not, they have a right to ask for a second opinion.

There are currently a small number of centres in the UK that specialize in the diagnosis and assessment of children and adolescents with social and communication disorders. Among these, one, which is one of the services run by the National Autistic Society, accepts referrals of adults of all ages as well as children. This centre also runs courses for professional workers. It is hoped that these will lead to the setting up of further specialist diagnostic centres that will be part of a network for the advancement of ideas on diagnostic methods.

Medical services for physical illnesses

As far as physical illnesses are concerned, children and adults with autistic disorders have access to the same NHS or private medical services, through referral by the family doctor, that are used by the general population. There are no specialized services available.

Psychiatric services

There are no specialist services for people with autistic disorders who develop psychiatric illnesses. They are treated as out- or in-patients by psychiatrists in the services for adults with psychiatric conditions or by the psychiatrists for those with learning difficulties. In general, the staff in the services for adults with learning difficulties have more experience with and understanding of autistic disorders.

Admission to an acute NHS or private hospital ward for adult psychiatric illness or for people with learning difficulties with disturbed behaviour can be a traumatic experience for someone with an autistic disorder. The illnesses of the other residents mean that events are unpredictable, at times even chaotic, which is the worst possible environment for someone with an autistic disorder. Treatment within the individual's own familiar environment, with medication if necessary, given by a psychiatrist who is familiar with autistic disorders, is the best solution if at all possible. Sometimes admission to a hospital is essential. It would help to reduce the problems if all staff in psychiatric establishments were to be given at least some training in the nature of autistic disorders and the needs of the people concerned, since all will, at some time in their careers, have to work with people with these conditions.

Some adults with autistic disorders who commit serious crimes as a result of their lack of understanding of social rules are sent to prison if the diagnosis is not recognized. Others are placed in the special hospitals or regional secure units. In 1994, the National Autistic Society collaborated with the Special Hospitals Authority, the government agency responsible for secure provision for mentally disordered offenders, in running a conference to raise awareness among the staff of the Special Hospitals. Early in 1996, the Society is to open a unit for adults with autistic disorders who need a secure placement and is working closely with the authorities involved in this field. This is a pioneering initiative, which, if successful, may lead to more units of this kind.

Dental services

There are no specialist dental services for children or adults with autistic disorders. They can be treated in the private or the remaining NHS dental practices available to everyone. Many health authorities provide a school dental service with mobile vans that visit schools, including those attended by children with autistic disorders. Some give treatment if the parents wish and some just do dental inspections.

As mentioned in Chapter 17, there are some dentists with a special interest in treating children or adults with learning difficulties, including autistic disorders. Some have special experience because they provide a service for a school, residential home or hospital that caters for children or adults with autistic disorders. Parents can find out about dentists with special expertise in their own area by making enquiries of other parents, the

Local Autistic Society and relevant local services, such as those for people with learning difficulties.

Clinical psychology

Clinical psychologists are employed by NHS trusts to work in services for children or for adults, for psychiatric conditions or for learning difficulties. Some work privately and may do sessions in schools, homes or day centres where there are people with autistic disorders.

Social services

The personal social services in England and Wales are managed by the local authority social services departments, which have a wide range of responsibilities. All that can be done here is to mention some of the functions that may be relevant for people with autistic disorders and their families. Parents should make direct enquiries to see if help for any particular problem is available, even if not mentioned in the following brief list.

It is useful for parents to inform the local social services that they have a child with a disability before they are in need of their help because those running the services like to be able to foresee future demands. Social workers can provide advice on the complex system of financial benefits to which people with disabilities and their carers are entitled and help families to obtain them. The local authority social services are also responsible for running a range of relevant day and residential services for adults and for the provision of respite care, practical help in the home, various kinds of equipment for use in the home, adaptations of the structure of the home if needed, travel to specialist facilities, leisure activities and holidays and for the provision of meals, as well as having an involvement with the care and protection of children. The social services should also be a source of information on voluntary bodies of all kinds from which help might be obtained.

The social services have a statutory duty to arrange for the assessment of the needs of people with disabilities as they approach the transition between school and adult life. For this reason, it is important for families with children with autistic disorders to contact the local social services while the children are still at school, if no social worker is already involved. The actual assessment of needs may be carried out by a social worker employed by the local social services or the social services may commission a social worker from another agency. The National Autistic Society has a specialized assessment service for this purpose.

The social services departments are now responsible for funding places in most types of residential, day and respite care, whether this is run by them or by some other agency. Financial constraints are severe for this also – another reason for parents to make contact in good time before an adult placement is needed.

Practical advice for parents

Parents can learn from books and papers some of the general principles of living and working with children with autistic disorders, but they need specific advice on how to adapt the ideas to their own child. This can be done most effectively if an experienced adviser regularly visits the child's home and bases suggestions on the child's behaviour in their everyday environment and on the resources available to the family.

In the early 1970s, a team of workers at the Institute of Psychiatry set up a programme of this kind to help parents improve their management strategies, using behavioural methods in a flexible way. This started as a research project but is now carried on as a clinical service within the National Health Service. The help given is highly valued by the parents receiving it but the programme has been copied in very few other areas of the country, though individual psychologists with an interest in autistic disorders do advise parents.

Many social workers in the social services would like to be able to work with individual families, giving emotional support

and practical help, but their other commitments make this difficult or impossible. In some areas, psychologists and other professionals working in the services for people with learning
difficulties do home visits and advise parents but the resources
for such intensive work are limited and insufficient time is available for much effective help to be given.

Local Autistic Societies provide the opportunity for parents
to meet each other and exchange ideas. They can also arrange
meetings with speakers who are experienced with the practical
problems. These formal and informal meetings of groups of
parents are one of the most valuable sources of support and help.
Some Local Societies employ outreach workers to help families
with information and advice.

For children attending schools, exchange of information and
advice between parents and teachers and cooperation with regard
to the child's daily programme is well worth the effort involved
in organizing regular communication.

The National and Local Autistic Societies organize courses,
meetings and all kinds of support for parents, as described later
in this chapter.

Pre-school units

Young children with autistic disorders benefit from attending
some kind of pre-school unit. Many playgroups or nursery
schools will accept children with disabilities. Even if, as usually
happens, the child with an autistic disorder does not voluntarily
mix with the other children, they gradually become accustomed
to the proximity of their age peers. At first, they may be distressed
by being in a group, or react with aggression to children who
approach them. This can usually be overcome if, initially, they
are allowed to be on their own, away from the others, while a
relationship with the staff is developed. They can then be led by
an adult they trust into closer contact with the other children.
At this pre-school stage, mixing with children without disabilities
often works well. There is no pressure to engage in tasks beyond
the child's capacity and very young children have not yet

developed the strong group feeling that can at a later age lead to rejection of those who are different.

In some areas, there are special pre-school units for observation and assessment of children with developmental delays of all kinds, or specifically for children with delay in language. If there is a choice between a specialized unit and an ordinary playgroup or nursery school, the decision must depend upon the individual child and their specific needs. A few of the schools for children with autistic disorders have nursery classes for pre-school children.

Educational services

All types of school, special and mainstream, state, voluntary and private, have accepted children with autistic disorders. Further Education Colleges also cater for some in their special needs or their mainstream courses.

There are a small number of schools, units or classes that specialize in the field, most being set up and run by National or Local Autistic Societies, some by local education authorities and a few by private organizations. These cater for only a small proportion of children with autistic disorders. Other special schools, particularly those for children with severe learning difficulties (SLD schools) take a large number, while some are in mainstream schools, with or without special support.

MAINSTREAM OR SPECIAL SCHOOL?

There is currently a division of opinion concerning education for children with disabilities. There is pressure from some quarters for education in mainstream schools for every child, regardless of the nature of their disability, in order to ensure equality of opportunity and to avoid the stigma of segregation. There is no doubt that very many, perhaps most, children with disabilities benefit from mainstream schooling with their age peers. However, the desire to include in mainstream education all children with specific or general learning difficulties is based on theory rather than knowledge and understanding of each individual child's real needs.

With regard to children with autistic disorders, the situation is complicated because they vary so widely in their levels of ability and their patterns of behaviour. It is often argued that all the children need normal role models, especially for developing social skills. It is suggested that the children cannot become sociable if they are educated together with other children who are equally socially impaired. There are some children among the more able who do well in mainstream schools, especially in some small voluntary or private schools that will take children with academic ability who have special needs. Some have enough insight to try to learn social rules by observing other children, though they make many mistakes and would benefit from specific teaching of social skills.

However, the majority of children with autistic disorders, because of the nature of their impairments, do not learn by copying their age peers. They learn social skills by rote if they are specifically taught by adults who are experienced in the appropriate teaching techniques. Apart from those with good academic ability, the children's pace and methods of learning school work differ markedly from those of other children, making it difficult for teachers to cope with such a diversity of need. This point is discussed in detail in the book by Rita Jordan and Stuart Powell, *Understanding and Teaching Children with Autism*. If the child has a non-teaching assistant, this may help them to integrate successfully but, if the child cannot join in with any of the lessons and has to be involved with their own special activities in class and playtime, there seems no point in continuing with mainstream education just for the sake of an ideal.

The other major problem is the attitude of other children. This has already been mentioned in Chapter 14 but is important enough to merit repetition in the context of the present chapter. Whereas young children usually accept those who are different, older children and adolescents tend to apply strong pressures to conform to group norms and are intolerant of those who do not fit in. This can lead to teasing and bullying if the child who is different is not protected by adult supervision. Much of this persecution occurs in the playground or before or after school, unobserved by the staff. The child concerned, because of the communication impairments, may never tell parents or teachers and just suffer in silence. If the child has never been diagnosed, teachers may be irritated by their stubbornness and lack of respect for those in authority and may be unsympathetic or even blame the child for any disturbance in the class. Some children have been desperately unhappy at mainstream school. Some survive but others develop reactive depression or other psychiatric disorders in adolescence. In my clinical experience, some adults carry the memory of miserable school days with them always and a very few have tried to revenge themselves in inappropriate ways.

The most reasonable approach is to acknowledge that a range of types of schools is required and that each individual child's needs should be assessed before deciding on their placement. The child's progress and emotional adjustment in the school should be monitored and changes made if necessary. There are some more able children with autistic disorders who can hold their own in mainstream schools and have made up their own minds that, despite all the difficulties, this is the type of education they want. Such children should be given every help and encouragement to stay in the school of their choice. Those who cannot cope, especially if they are unhappy, should be found places in special schools. This should not be regarded as an all or none decision.

It works well if there is cooperation between a mainstream school and a special school so that children from the latter who would benefit can attend for specific sessions with the mainstream children. They may eventually achieve full integration but this should not be forced if it is not in the child's best interests. If there is a partnership between a mainstream and a special school, the mainstream children spend some time in the special school to broaden their understanding of disability as well as helping the children with special needs.

TYPES OF SPECIAL SCHOOLS

Among the special schools, those for children with emotional and behavioural disturbance (EBD schools) are the least likely to be suitable for children with autistic disorders. There are some exceptions where the staff are able to provide for these children's special needs but, in most, the interests of the other children conflict too markedly with those who have autistic disorders. With the more able children, there is also the possibility that they will learn, in a naive fashion, delinquent attitudes and activities from their schoolmates. Bullying is also a problem in some schools of this kind.

Schools for children with language disorders often have some with autistic disorders among their pupils. This placement can work well and is worth considering for more able children but it is not necessarily appropriate for the children with marked social and communication impairments in addition to delayed language development.

There are some schools that specialize in teaching children with hearing or visual impairments or dyslexia or physical disabilities. Children with autistic disorders who also have one or more of these other disabilities may be placed in such schools. This can occur because the autistic disorder has not been recognized or is considered to be secondary to the sensory or physical disability. The chances are high that such placements will be unsatisfactory. Whatever other disability a child may have, if the triad of impairments is also present, that is the major factor determining the educational approach that is needed.

The schools for children with moderate (MLD) or with severe learning difficulties (SLD schools), especially the latter, tend to have larger proportions of children with autistic disorders among their pupils than any other type of school. This type of placement is appropriate for some of the children who have learning difficulties, especially if some of the staff are interested in and have training in teaching children with autistic disorders and the school programme is sufficiently structured and organized.

Parents of children who have typical autistic behaviour and

no physical signs of disability but who have severe or profound learning difficulties are often worried and confused when it is suggested that their child should attend the local SLD school. Many would prefer to have them educated in schools that specialize in autistic disorders. They are further distressed by the physical disabilities of many children in SLD schools. The fact is that there are few specialist schools and it is unlikely, to put it mildly, that there will ever be enough to cater for all children with autistic disorders. The most sensible solution is for some staff in all SLD schools and other special schools that may take children with autistic disorders to undertake training in methods of teaching these children. More distance learning courses, like the pioneering one run by the University of Birmingham School of Education, are required. It would be helpful for schools to experiment with different ways of organizing teaching for children with autistic disorders to see if special units, special groups within classes or some other system works best. Care has to be taken to ensure that resources are not removed from other children with special needs. Ideally, all the different specific impairments to be found among children with all kinds of developmental disorders should be analyzed and appropriately addressed in their educational programmes. Teachers who understand the basic principles of teaching children with autistic disorders are in a better position to apply their knowledge to other disabilities. In areas where there are no schools with a special interest in autistic disorders, parents may be effective in bringing about change if they act together to apply pressure.

The few schools specializing in the education of children with autistic disorders that do exist are the pioneers in developing methods of teaching. They are most appropriate for children with potential skills who are unable to cope in other types of school, often because of their behaviour. The most able children, including those who have the pattern of Asperger's syndrome, who are unhappy and not making progress in mainstream school, present a special problem. They require to be taught with the methods that suit other children with autistic disorders, but are too advanced in schoolwork to fit into most of the specialist schools. A school has now been set up by a private body for children of this kind and it is to be hoped that others will follow.

The Camphill Movement, based on the ideas of Rudolf Steiner, runs some day and residential schools in the UK for children of all ages who have special needs. These accept children with autistic disorders among those with other disabilities. There are also a number of centres for adolescents. The gentle but organized regime suits some of the children very well. They enjoy the occasions for simple ceremonies that mark the passage of the days and some become skilled at the practical tasks that are taught, such as weaving, gardening, baking and woodwork. Not all can fit in with the philosophy of group living but those who are able to do so benefit from the life-style.

RESIDENTIAL SCHOOLING

There are still some residential schools, including those that specialize in autistic disorders, but local education authorities prefer to place children in day schools whenever possible. In general, parents of younger children with autistic disorders also prefer day schooling, though they may have to resolve the dilemma of choosing between a local school offering a less suitable educational programme and one with a more appropriate programme where the child would have to board.

Residential placements tend to be considered by the education authority only when there are special circumstances. These include educational reasons, such as the child requiring a consistent 24-hour programme that can be provided only in a residential school, or family situations that make it difficult or impossible for the child to live at home, such as severe disturbance of behaviour in an adolescent.

Most residential schools offer weekly boarding but there are a very few that provide an educational programme for 52 weeks of the year for children with autistic disorders. It would be desirable to increase this provision for adolescents whose families are finding it hard to cope. Young people in this situation, including those who dominate their own families, suffer as much as their parents and siblings do from the often chaotic home situation

and would obtain great benefit from a consistent programme of
education and leisure throughout the year.

UNORTHODOX EDUCATIONAL APPROACHES

Claims have been made concerning the results of several unorthodox educational methods, including Daily Life Therapy at the
Higashi schools in Boston, USA and Tokyo, the Waldon
approach, behaviour modification as used by Ivar Lovaas, Feuer-
stein's Mediated Learning, Low Intrusion Teaching and Gentle
Teaching. None has been evaluated by independent research
workers. There is much overlap among these methods and many
similarities with more orthodox approaches. None has anything
completely new to offer, although each has some useful ideas.
The TEACCH approach developed in North Carolina is particularly valuable as a method of designing organized but individualized programmes.

The staff in the National Autistic Society schools study the
different systems and take from each whatever proves useful and
discard whatever is of no value or possibly harmful. The children
vary in their responses to different educational methods so it is
appropriate to have a range of techniques available.

ASSESSMENT OF EDUCATIONAL NEEDS AND 'STATEMENTING'

Local Education Authorities (LEAs) and the governing bodies of
all maintained schools have responsibilities towards all children
with special educational needs, as set out in the 1993 Education
Act. It is interesting to note that, according to the Code of Practice
on this subject issued by the Department for Education and
Employment, it has been estimated that about 20 per cent of the
school population will have special educational needs at some
time during their school career. In each school a teacher or a
team of teachers has the role of Special Educational Needs (SEN)
coordinator.

The Department for Education has published a *Code of*

Practice on the Identification and Assessment of Special Educational Needs. This recommends a staged response to children's special educational needs, each successive stage bringing in more specialist advice and help. The process can finish at any stage, depending on the individual child's needs. The highest stage, for children with the most needs, is the Statutory Assessment, which may lead to a Statement of Special Educational Needs. This is made when the LEA decides that all the special help the child needs cannot reasonably be provided within the resources normally available to the school.

A local educational authority can assess the needs of a child even when under two years old. After two years of age, a statutory assessment can be made on a pre-school child and a Statement of Special Educational Needs made if considered necessary. The parents and all professionals involved with the child are asked to contribute to the evidence for the statutory assessment.

If a child is 'statemented' (a new word coined for this process) their special needs must be met by additional help at a mainstream school or by placement in a special school. Children who have such statements made are entitled to education in mainstream or special schools or in a college of further education.

This is only a brief outline of some aspects of the process of assessing special educational needs and 'statementing'. Much more detailed information is available in the Department for Education and Employment's booklet *Special Educational Needs; A Guide for Parents*. The most important points are as follows. Parents can initiate an assessment of needs and can do so in the pre-school years as well as at any time in the child's school life. Parents must be asked to supply information and their views on the child's needs and can submit reports from professional workers if they wish. Parents can go with their child to any assessment although the professionals can ask to see the child alone at some stage. In discussions with the LEA, parents can arrange for a 'Named Person' to help them represent their views. Parents can express their views on the 'proposed Statement' that is sent to them before the statement is finalized. If a statement is made, parents have a right to say which school they wish their child to attend. The LEA has to agree if it is a state school but with certain provisos that are vague enough to allow the LEA to disagree if they so wish. If the parents prefer a non-maintained or independent school, the LEA have to consider this but have no legal duty to place a child in such a school. If they disagree with the final statement, or if the LEA decides the child does not need a statement and the parents think they do, parents have the right to appeal to the Special Educational Needs Tribunal, which is an independent body.

It is essential for parents of children with autistic disorders to find out as much as they can concerning the provisions for special educational needs and to consider carefully how to make best use of the services available for their own child. For school-age children at mainstream school, the SEN coordinator at the school should be approached to help with the search for information. For pre-school children, health visitors, doctors or social workers should be consulted.

The above outlines the situation as it is at the time of writing. It is very possible that changes will occur, so parents need to make sure they have the latest information.

THE NATIONAL CURRICULUM

The Department for Education and Employment states that all children with special needs have a right to a broad and well-balanced curriculum that should include as much work as possible under the National Curriculum. In their book on education for children with autistic disorders, Rita Jordan and Stuart Powell include a most perceptive discussion of the relevance of the National Curriculum to these children. They make the point that teaching self-care and practical and social skills should have a high priority for the many children with autistic disorders who cannot acquire these basic life skills without special help. They also ask the pertinent question of whether learning subjects such as history or a foreign language are really a priority for those pupils who have severe social and communication impairments and bizarre stereotyped behaviour. The authors' suggestions for a practical approach to curriculum planning for the children are sensible and helpful.

Speech and language therapy

The NHS trusts employ speech and language therapists. Within the trusts, they can undertake community-based work, mainly in paediatric clinics, or work with children who have special needs, mainly those with learning difficulties including autistic disorders, or work in the adult speech and language therapy service. Independent special schools, including those for children with autistic disorders, may employ their own speech and language therapists. Some speech therapists work privately.

Physiotherapy and occupational therapy

NHS trusts also employ these therapists. Some of the practitioners work privately.

Music and other special therapies

The various specialized therapies mentioned in Chapter 17 (music, aroma, relaxation, massage, dance, drama etc) are carried out by therapists who work privately and who can be employed by the services for people with disabilities, including those with autistic disorders, on a sessional basis. The same is true for instructors of horse-riding, physical education etc, all of whom can contribute to improving the skills and quality of life for people with autistic disorders.

Occupational services

The majority of the most able people with autistic disorders can work in open employment. A proportion of them settle in jobs that are well below their academic ability and qualifications. This is usually due to their poor social skills and lack of the planning ability and flexibility required for higher level occupations. The low level of work may be disappointing to parents but, if it suits the individual concerned, the fact that they are independent should be seen as a success. Disapproval should be avoided so that the self-esteem of the person is not damaged.

The National Autistic Society in partnership with the Employers' Forum has recently set up a scheme for finding work for more able people with autistic disorders and employing specialist job coaches to support them. At the time of writing, various organizations are cooperating in making suitable posts available to individuals on the scheme.

A large proportion of adults with autistic disorders are unable to work in open employment even with support and need sheltered occupations. The most usual placement is in day Social Education Centres for adults with learning difficulties run by local social service authorities. This may work well but often the special needs of those with autistic disorders are not provided for and problems arise. The centres tend to be noisy and full of movement. Little or none of the work available may be suitable and often there is too little structure to the day for people with autistic disorders. In some centres, the staff have managed to organize a separate programme for those who cannot fit in with the sociable people, which is a solution to be encouraged.

There are a few day centres set up by the National or Local Autistic Societies. Some operate in association with residential homes but may have a few places for day attenders from the local area.

Centres for sheltered work and leisure activities with programmes suitable for adults with autistic disorders are few in number and an unknown number of adults, after leaving school, have no form of occupation and stay at home all day, perhaps watching the same videos over and over again or engaging in other repetitive activities. It would be most desirable for more opportunities for sheltered work and other activities to be made available. Apart from all the other advantages, this would reduce to some extent the need for residential care.

Respite care

The local social services are able to pay for periods of respite care for children and adults with special needs. Some charitable bodies can use money for this purpose and parents can themselves pay for some types of placements if they can afford to do so. Breaks from caring for parents and other carers can alleviate the pressures of living with a child or adult with an autistic disorder. Places for short-term care are available in some local authority, voluntary body and privately-run residential homes. In practice, financial constraints and shortage of suitable placements limit the use that families can make of this service.

In some areas, the system has been set up of linking families who have children with disabilities with other families willing to provide occasional care, perhaps for a half day, overnight, a weekend or even longer. This can work very well but the disturbed behaviour and unusual needs of children with autistic disorders make for problems in finding link families who are able to offer suitable care.

Residential care for adults

The most able autistic adults organize their own lives. Others in the more able group can live on their own but need some regular support to make sure that daily needs are being met and to help solve any problems that may arise. Social workers from the local social services or from voluntary bodies may provide this form of assistance.

Adults with autistic disorders who cannot live independently, most of them never diagnosed, can be found in every type of sheltered accommodation. These may be run by NHS trusts, local social services or voluntary or private bodies, especially homes or units for people with learning difficulties. This sometimes works well if the staff understand the autistic impairments and the environment is organized enough to suit the individuals with autistic disorders. Problems arise if there is too little structure and if the residents have to do much planning for themselves.

A very few homes specially for adults with autistic disorders have been set up in different areas by each of the types of agencies mentioned above. The National and Local Autistic Societies run specialist residential homes in various parts of the UK. The first such homes were for 20 or more adults. Currently, the National and Local Autistic Societies are working in conjunction with Housing Associations to develop small homes within local communities. However, the larger homes or groups of small living units in their own grounds are still needed for adults who have severe levels of disability and behaviour disturbance, especially if they need space and tend to be distressed by the proximity of other people except in carefully organized situations.

The National and Local Autistic Societies are becoming aware of the special needs of the more able adults with autistic disorders, including those with Asperger's syndrome. The Societies are developing different kinds of residential accommodation to suit different requirements. Among these are small group homes or individual flats where the residents care for themselves. These are each associated with a fully staffed home and the staff from this home provides regular supervision for those living more independently. These more independent people have the security of knowing where they can turn for help at any time it is needed. Residents can live at first in the fully staffed home and then move on to more independence if they are able to cope.

As well as schools, the Camphill Movement has set up various training units, residential homes and sheltered villages for people with learning difficulties and some adults with autistic disorders have settled happily in such placements, though they are not suitable for those who cannot tolerate the type of group living that the Rudolf Steiner philosophy encourages.

How to find and evaluate services

Most of the effort involved in finding the right services for children and adults with autistic disorders has to come from the parents although they can obtain information and advice from the Advice Service of the National Autistic Society. Many Local Autistic Societies can also provide information about what is available locally. Parents should contact the local social services because they run some of the relevant services and can give information about other sources of help, though they are less likely than the Societies to know about specialist provision for autistic disorders outside those in the local area. Parents should find out as much as they can from other parents who have experience of different services. They should also obtain information from professionals in the field. For special therapies available from those who work privately, the relevant professional college or association should be able to provide information on how to find qualified local practitioners.

It is essential for parents to visit schools, homes and other services and to be armed with a list of questions. It is necessary to persevere until the queries are answered satisfactorily. Suggestions for essential questions are given in publications obtainable from the National Autistic Society.

Most parents know their own child better than anyone else. It is very useful for parents, teachers or carers to exchange information and to learn from each other. Parents naturally want the best for their child and it is right for them to try to obtain this. However, hard though this is, it helps to retain a sense of proportion and to avoid making demands on the services that, with the best will in the world, are impossible to meet. Knowing when to apply pressure and when to hold back requires cool judgement, which is difficult when strong emotions are involved. In such situations it may help to talk about the problems with someone who is sympathetic but who can be objective. Some compromises are necessary but this must not mean that the children and adults with autistic disorders have a poor quality of life.

The role of voluntary societies

Voluntary Societies have a special role to play for families with children with all kinds of disabilities and in helping professionals in the field as well. Parents who are members obtain various kinds of help but many also gain from the satisfaction of working with others to initiate and improve services for their children.

THE NATIONAL AUTISTIC SOCIETY

The National Autistic Society, originally called the Society for Autistic Children, was formed by a group of parents in 1962. They came together for an inaugural meeting as a result of a talk on the radio on 'Woman's Hour' by one of their number, Helen Green Allison. It was decided to invite professional workers as well as parents to join. It was soon realized that there were many children who were not classically autistic in the way Kanner described but who had similar needs, so the membership was expanded to include their parents. In time, as the membership grew and parents of older people joined, the needs of adults were recognized and the name was changed to the National Autistic Society. The structure now comprises the National Society and a large number of Local Autistic Societies almost all of which are affiliated to the National body.

The first commitment of the newly formed society was to set up a school for children with autism. This aim was achieved in 1964, when Sybil Elgar opened the first of the Society schools, which is now named after her. After this, more schools were opened by the National Society and by some Local Societies. Then attention began to be focused on adults. Sybil Elgar was the pioneer in this field also and set up, in 1974, Somerset Court, the first of the National Society's residential communities for adults. Other residential homes have since been opened by the National and by Local Societies. Joint meetings are organized for staff and members of management and support committees of the schools and adult centres.

Over the years, the size of the National Society has grown steadily and the work it undertakes has expanded. Some of the services it provides have been mentioned already under various headings but will be brought together here. One invaluable aspect of its functions is the Advice Service, which gives information and advice to parents over the telephone and by letter. This service is used by large numbers of parents every day and is greatly appreciated. Another department provides general information on all aspects of autistic disorders for professionals and interested parents. A Society journal and a newsletter are published regularly. The Society also publishes booklets and leaflets on a variety of subjects, keeps a list of other relevant books and papers and has for sale a stock of books from other publishers that are of particular interest to parents and professionals in the field. Keeping the general public informed about autistic conditions through the media helps to raise awareness and sympathy.

The National Autistic Society runs occasional one or two day courses for parents of young children. Where possible, arrangements are made for childminding so that the child with an autistic disorder and brothers and sisters can be cared for while the parents attend the talks and discussions. The National headquarters office and regional offices have staff who can give parents information and advice on educational and residential provision and where to find practical help.

Courses on different aspects of autism are run for professionals or for mixed audiences of parents and professionals. The Society aims to educate administrators from health, education and social services as well as workers in the caring professions.

The Society works to encourage the setting up of services by statutory authorities and has a special interest in increasing cooperation with central government and local authorities and developing joint projects of all kinds for children and adults. Some joint projects have already been started.

A number of special services have been initiated and funded by the National Society. The Centre for Social and Communication Disorders at Elliot House in Bromley provides a diagnostic and assessment service for people of all ages, runs professional training courses and is involved in research on methods of diagnosis, assessment and classification of autistic spectrum disorders. The Autism Research Unit is located in the University of Sunderland School of Health Sciences. One of its activities is the compiling of a computer data base containing references to books and papers on autism and allied subjects, names of professionals in the field and details of research projects. Another is to organize the annual Durham conference for professional workers. Family Service Workers who provide outreach help and support for families in their areas are being appointed in different parts of the UK. Development Officers have been appointed in different regional offices of the National Society to work with local societies, local authorities, trusts and private bodies to examine needs and identify resources. They also try to ensure that local authorities meet their statutory responsibilities with regard to autistic disorders and maintain high standards in the services provided. National Society Project Officers, funded by local health and/or social services, are appointed to undertake specific tasks in relation to developing services for autistic people.

The Supported Employment Scheme has been previously described in this chapter. The development of a home providing secure accommodation for people with autistic disorders who commit offences is also mentioned above. A system of accreditation for schools and adult establishments accepting people with autistic disorders has been set up. A panel of advisers has been assembled to assess the ethical aspects of research projects for which the Society's help in finding subjects has been requested.

In addition to all these functions, the staff of the National Society keep up with the latest developments in the field. They are also developing links with other similar societies throughout the world. Help has been given to groups in other countries setting up schools and other services. Exchanges of staff working in related establishments and other exchange visits have been arranged. The National Society is a member of the association of autistic societies throughout Europe, known as Autism Europe.

As it is a voluntary body, the Society has an active fundraising department in order to support all these activities.

LOCAL AUTISTIC SOCIETIES

The system of a national body with affiliated local societies allows for coherent policies at national level but preserves the closer and more informal relationships at local level. The latter are the source of so much of the enthusiasm a voluntary body must have among its members if it is to be effective. The National Society has set up and continues to facilitate Regional Forums in which representatives of the Local Autistic Societies in each region meet together to exchange ideas and to discuss plans.

Local Autistic Societies provide a forum for parents to meet each other and to talk with professionals, formally or informally. Some organize social events, including activities that involve the whole family. A number of Local Societies have set up libraries to lend books, toys and other equipment, such as computers, to members. Some employ their own outreach workers to support families. Fundraising is always a major activity and some events can be social occasions for members and local residents. Local contacts can be useful both for fundraising and the development of local services. Some Local Autistic Societies have set up their own schools, adult residential homes, resource centres, or other services.

OTHER VOLUNTARY BODIES

Autistic disorders can occur together with a variety of other developmental disorders. There are associations for many different specific conditions and parents of children with autistic disorders may find it helpful to contact or to join other relevant groups as well as the National and Local Autistic Society. To give just a few examples, there are associations or support groups for parents of children with tuberose sclerosis, attention disorder and hyperactive disorder, fragile X and children with hearing and visual impairments. Some parents with very able children with autistic disorders have joined the association for gifted children. The precise names and other details of relevant voluntary bodies can be obtained from the Information department of the National Autistic Society.

Postscript

Those of us who live and/or work with children and adults with autistic disorders have to try to enter their world, since they cannot find their way into ours. We need to learn to comprehend and empathize with autistic experiences in order to find ways to help each individual cope with a system of social rules that is alien to them. The reward for the effort involved is a deeper understanding of human social interaction and an appreciation of the wonder of child development. The key to autism is the key to the nature of human life.

Reading list

The National Autistic Society keeps updated lists of relevant books and papers in journals and also publishes some booklets and leaflets. Details can be obtained from the address given at the end.

Books

So many interesting and useful books have now been published concerning autistic spectrum disorders and related subjects that it is impossible to give an exhaustive list. The titles mentioned here include all the books referred to in the text together with a few others covering the same topics.

PRACTICAL GUIDANCE

Aarons, M. and Gittens, T. *The Handbook of Autism*. London: Routledge, 1992.
(Information on causes, diagnosis, education, development of communication and an objective view of 'alternative treatments'.)
Carr, J. *Helping Your Handicapped Child*, 2nd edition. Harmondsworth, Middlesex: Penguin Books, 1995.

(Practical guidance for parents of children with learning difficulties.)

Howlin, P. *Autism in Adolescents and Adults*. London: Routledge, 1996.

(Practical advice mainly concerned with the more able adolescents and adults, including those with Asperger's syndrome.)

Jordan, R. and Powell, S. *Understanding and Teaching Children with Autism*. Chichester: Wiley, 1995.

(Theory and practice of teaching children with autistic disorders.)

Morgan, H. *Adults with Autism*. Cambridge: Cambridge University Press, 1996.

(Proposals for models of good practice in the services for adults with autistic disorders.)

McKernon, T. and Mortlock, J. *Autism Focus*. St Leonards on Sea: Outset Publishing, 1995.

(A training manual for staff working with adults with autistic disorders.)

CLINICAL DESCRIPTIONS, RESEARCH AND THEORIES

Baron-Cohen, S. *Mind Blindness: An Essay on Autism and Theory of Mind*. London: MIT, 1995.

(An interesting discussion of the development of 'theory of mind' in children and the implications for understanding autism.)

Baron-Cohen, S. and Bolton, P. *Autism: The Facts*. London: Oxford University Press, 1993.

(A clear explanation of autism for parents and carers.)

Frith, U. *Autism: Explaining the Enigma*. Oxford: Blackwell, 1989.

(Ideas on the nature of autism based on results of psychological research.)

Frith, U. (Editor) *Autism and Asperger Syndrome*. Cambridge: Cambridge University Press, 1991.

(Chapters by different authors on the nature of Asperger's syndrome and its relationship to Kanner's autism and other autistic spectrum disorders. A translation into English of Asperger's first paper on his syndrome is included.)

- Happé, F. *Autism: An Introduction to Psychological Theory*. London: UCL, 1994.
(A clear discussion of theories concerning the psychological impairments in autism.)
Kanner, L. *Childhood Psychosis: Initial Studies and New Insights*. Washington, DC: Winston, 1973.
(A collection of Kanner's papers on autism, including the original one in which he described 11 children with the typical syndrome. The sequence of papers shows the development of and changes in Kanner's ideas on the subject.)

INDIVIDUAL HISTORIES

Grandin, T. and Scariano, M. M. *Emergence: Labelled Autistic*. Tunbridge Wells: Costello, 1986.
(The life story of a woman with autism who has become independent and runs her own successful business.)
Park, C. C. *The Siege*. London: Little, Brown, 1990.
(An account of her daughter's development by the mother of a more able young woman with autism.)

SPECIAL SKILLS IN INDIVIDUALS WITH AUTISTIC DISORDERS

Selfe, L. *Nadia: A Case of Extraordinary Drawing Ability in an Autistic Child*. London: Academic Press, 1977.
(The drawings of a young child with autism and a discussion of the nature of her special skill.)
Treffert, D. A. *Extraordinary People*. London: Bantam Press, 1989.
(Case histories and discussions of people with remarkable special skills in music, art, calendar calculation etc.)
Wiltshire, S. *Cities*. London: Dent, 1989.
(The detailed architectural drawings of a boy with autism.)

THE MYTHS OF 'WOLF' CHILDREN

Clarke, A. M. and Clarke, A. D. B. (Editors) *Early Experience: Myth and Evidence*. London: Open Books, 1976.
(Case histories and scientific discussions of the effects of early experiences, including isolation from others from an early age.)
Lane, H. *The Wild Boy of Aveyron*. London: Allen and Unwin, 1977.
(Translations of J. M. G. Itard's reports on Victor, the 'wild boy', and an account of the way Itard's methods of teaching Victor have influenced development of education for those with hearing impairments or learning difficulties. Victor's behaviour was that of a child with typical autism, although the author of this book did not recognize this!)

CAUSES AND NEUROPATHOLOGY

Bauman, M. and Kemper, T. (Editors) *The Neurobiology of Autism*. Baltimore: Johns Hopkins, 1994.
(Current research in many aspects of the biological basis of autism.)
Gillberg, C. and Coleman, M. *The Biology of the Autistic Syndromes*. London: Mac Keith Press, 1992.
(An overview of the many biological conditions that can be associated with autistic disorders and the medical aspects of investigation and treatment.)
Sacks, O. *Awakenings*. London: Pan Books, 1982.
(An account of the victims of the epidemic of encephalitis lethargica following the First World War and their treatment with anti-Parkinson medication. The overlap with the behaviour seen in autistic disorders is striking and suggests that the neuropathologies of the two conditions are related.)

EDUCATION: GUIDANCE ON THE 'STATEMENTING' PROCESS

Department for Education. *Code of Practice on the Identification and Assessment of Special Educational Needs*. London: DFE, 1994.
Department for Education. *Special Educational Needs; A Guide for Parents*. London: DFE, 1994.

INTERNATIONAL DIAGNOSTIC CRITERIA

American Psychiatric Association. *Diagnostic and Statistical Manual*. Washington DC: APA. DSM III, 1980; DSM III-R, 1987; DSM IV, 1994.
World Health Organisation. *International Statistical Classification of Diseases and Related Health Problems*. Geneva: WHO. ICD 8, 1967; ICD 9, 1977; ICD 10, 1992.
World Health Organisation. *The ICD-10 Classification of Mental and Behavioural Disorders: Diagnostic Criteria for Research*. Geneva: WHO, 1993.
(These manuals give the diagnostic criteria decided on by committees of professional workers in the field. They are useful for comparative research and statistics but each edition inevitably lags behind the most advanced thinking in the field so should not be used rigidly as a basis for clinical diagnosis and decisions about services needed by individuals.)

THE 'TEACCH' SERIES

Eric Schopler and Gary Mesibov of the TEACCH Division of the University of North Carolina, Chapel Hill, have edited a series of multi-authored books on many different aspects of autistic spectrum disorders. Further volumes will be published in the future. Details of the books in this series can be obtained from the National Autistic Society. They are mainly directed at professional workers but are of interest to parents.

The TEACCH division also runs courses on their method of structured and organized education and occupational training. These take place in many different countries, including the UK. Details can be obtained from the National Autistic Society.

Booklets

These are the booklets published by the National Autistic Society that are mentioned in the text. Other titles are given in the 'Publications' booklet.
Approaches to Autism (1993)
(A guide to some of the different approaches suggested for the education or 'treatment' of children and adults with autistic disorders. Brief descriptions are given for information only. No recommendations are made.)
Managing Feeding Difficulties in Children with Autism (1991)
(Practical guidelines for staff working with people with autistic disorders on a wide range of problems connected with eating)
Publications (1995)
(A list of books, booklets, papers, leaflets and videos available through the NAS.)

Journal

Communication
(The journal of the National Autistic Society, published three times a year. It contains news of developments in the field in research and practice. It is also a forum for parents and professionals to share ideas and experiences.)

References to papers

It is not possible, for reasons of space, to give references to all the papers in the medical, psychological and educational literature relevant to the material in this book. The following list includes only the work of authors specifically mentioned in the text.

Asperger, H. (1944) 'Die autistischen psychopathen im kindes-alter' *Archiv für Psychiatrie und Nervenkrankheiten*, 117, 76–136.

Asperger, H. (1979) 'Problems of infantile autism' *Communication*, 13, 45–52.

Baron-Cohen, S., Cox, A., Baird, G., Swettenham, J., Nightingale, N., Morgan, K., Drew, A., and Charman, T. (1996) 'Psychological markers in the detection of autism in infancy in a large population' *British Journal of Psychiatry* (in press)

Bolton, P., MacDonald, H., Pickles, A., Rios, P., Goode, S., Crowson, M., Bailey, A., and Rutter, M. (1994) 'A case-control family history study of autism' *Journal of Child Psychology and Psychiatry*, 35, 877–900.

Bowler, B. (1994) '"Theory of mind" in Asperger's syndrome' *Journal of Child Psychology and Psychiatry*, 33, 877–894.

Ehlers, S. and Gillberg, C. (1993) 'The epidemiology of Asperger syndrome: A total population study' *Journal of Child Psychology and Psychiatry*, 34, 1327–1350.

Gillberg, C. (1983) 'Psychotic behaviour in children and young adults in a mental handicap hostel' *Acta Psychiatrica Scandinavica*, 68, 351–358.

Gillberg, C. (1992) 'The Emmanuel Miller Memorial Lecture 1991. Autism and autistic-like conditions: subclasses among disorders of empathy' *Journal of Child Psychology and Psychiatry*, 33, 813–842.

Gillberg, I. C. and Gillberg, C. (1989) 'Asperger syndrome: some epidemiological considerations' *Journal of Child Psychology and Psychiatry*, 30, 631–638.

Gillberg, C., Persson, E., Grufman, M. and Themner, U. (1986) 'Psychiatric disorders in mildly and severely mentally retarded urban children and adolescents: epidemiological aspects' *British Journal of Psychiatry*, 149, 68–74.

Gillberg, C., Rasmussen, P., Carlstrom, G., Svenson, B., and Waldenstrom, E. (1982) 'Perceptual, motor and attentional deficits in six-year-old children: epidemiological aspects' *Journal of Child Psychology and Psychiatry*, 12, 131–144.

Reading list

Gray, C., (1995) 'Teaching children with autism to read social situations' *In* K. A. Quill (Ed.) *Teaching Children with Autism Strategies to Enhance Communication and Socialization.* London: International Thomson Publications.

Haslam, J. (1809) 'Cases of insane children' *Observations on Madness and Melancholy.* London: Haydon, pp. 185–206.

Howlin, P. (1980) 'The home treatment of autistic children' *In* L. A. Hersov, M. Berger, and R. Nichol (Eds.) *Language and Language Disorders in Children.* Oxford: Pergamon Press.

Kanner, L. (1943) 'Autistic disturbances of affective contact' *Nervous Child*, 2, 217–250.

Kanner, L. (1946) 'Irrelevant and metaphorical language in early infantile autism' *American Journal of Psychiatry*, 103, 242–246.

Kolvin, I. (1971) 'Studies in the childhood psychoses: I. Diagnostic criteria and classification' *British Journal of Psychiatry*, 118, 381–384.

Lister Brook, S., and Bowler, D. (1992) 'Autism by another name? Semantic and pragmatic impairments in children' *Journal of Autism and Developmental Disorders*, 22, 61–82.

Maudsley, H. (1867) 'Insanity of early life' *In, The Physiology and Pathology of the Mind, First edition.* New York: Appleton, pp. 259–293.

Newson, E. (1983) 'Pathological demand-avoidance syndrome' *Communication*, 17, 3–8.

Oliver, C. (1993) 'Self-injurious behaviour: from response to strategy' *In* C. Kiernon (Ed.) *Research to Practice? Implications of Research on the Challenging Behaviour of People with Learning Disability.* Clevedon: BILD.

Rutter, M. (1968) 'Concepts of autism: a review of research' *Journal of Child Psychology and Psychiatry*, 9, 1–25.

Tantam, D. (1988) 'Lifelong eccentricity and social isolation: I. Psychiatric, social and forensic aspects' *British Journal of Psychiatry*, 153, 777–782.

Wing, L. (1993) 'The definition and prevalence of autism: a review' *European Child and Adolescent Psychiatry*, 2, 61–74.

Wing, L. and Gould, J. (1979) 'Severe impairments of social interaction and associated abnormalities in children:

epidemiology and classification' *Journal of Autism and Childhood Schizophrenia*, 9, 11–29.

Witmer, L. (1919–22) 'Don: A curable case of arrested development due to a fear psychosis in a three-year-old infant' *Psychological Clinics*, 13, 97–111.

Address of the NAS
The National Autistic Society
276 Willesden Lane
London
NW2 5RB

Telephone 0181 451 1114
Fax 0181 451 5865

Addresses of Local Autistic Societies can be obtained from the NAS headquarters.

Index

abuse, 118
Act of Parliament, 1971, 128
adolescence, 59, 149–52, 162–8
adulthood, 59, 153–4, 168–77
affection, 93–5
aggression, 56, 108–10, 142, 163
agility, 49
allergies, 143
aloofness, 35–6, 61, 182
anger, 108
anxiety, 53–4
appearance, 27
aromatherapy, 196
Asperger, Hans, 19, 20–1, 25, 49,
    66, 73, 75, 83, 158, 163, 164,
    165, 177
Asperger's syndrome, 20, 21, 29, 34,
    40, 47, 61, 63, 155–6, 163–4
attachment to objects see objects,
    attachment to
attention span, 54, 73, 116, 140,
    160
autism
    age of onset, 62–3
    defined, 20, 61
    history, 17–23

babies, 32–4, 146–8
baby talk, 34

backward chaining, 129, 136
Baron-Cohen, Simon, 33, 81
bath fears, 119, 120–1
Bauman, Margaret, 81
behaviour, 21–3, 28, 32–59, 156
    after 5 years old, 37–8, 58–9
    babyhood, 32–4, 146–8
    criminal, 175–6
    delinquent, 175–6
    difficult, 104
    early infantile, 19
    embarrassing, 57, 116–8
    immature, 65
    inappropriate, 56–8, 103–27,
        149–50
    management, 104–5, 193
    over-formal, 37–8
    patterns, 19, 27, 29, 34
    social, 20–1
beta-blockers, 110–11
birth complications, 79–80
Bolton, Patrick, 79
Bowler, Dermot, 72
brain, 22, 67, 80–1
brothers see siblings

Camberwell study, 21, 25, 61
Camphill Movement, 212, 219
catatonia, 174–5

causes, 24, 78–83
change, resistance to, 46, 73, 99–102, 106, 124, 134–5
Clarke, A.M. *and* Clarke, A.D.B., 77
clinical psychology, 204
clothing, 52, 115, 137
clubs, 166
clumsiness, 49
Communication (journal of the National Autistic Society), 180
communication, 27, 38–43, 97–8, 105, 106, 144
  non-verbal, 25, 42–3
  verbal *see* speech and language
community care, 62
computers, 55, 139, 151, 161
consistency, 94, 107
contraception, 152, 167
co-operation, 133–4, 150
co-ordination, 49, 73, 141, 161, 196
Cornelia de Lange syndrome, 70
counselling, 172, 193, 197–8
criminal behaviour, 175–6
cuddling *see* physical contact
'curative treatments', 199–200

dangers, unawareness of, 53, 122, 141
day centres, 153, 170, 198
deafness, 42–3, 70–1
delinquent behaviour, 175–6
dentist, 145, 192, 203–4
dependence, 185
depression, 74, 111, 172
deprivation, 76–7
desensitization, 119–20
destructiveness, 56, 112–3, 178
  self-destructiveness, 45, 113–5, 152
diagnosis and assessment, 27–31, 66, 67, 74–6, 156, 182, 188, 189–90, 191, 193, 201–2
diet, 143
disability
  acceptance of, 165

  attitudes to, 184, 208–9
  awareness of, 164–6
  understanding of, 165
doctor, 145, 188
dogs, 121
domination, 163–4
drawing, 55
dressing, 136–7
drinking, 53
Downs syndrome *see* mongolism
drugs, 111–12, 115

echolalia, 38–9, 72, 133
echopraxia, 50
education, 87, 150, 167–8, 194–5
educational
  needs, assessment of, 213–5
  psychologists, 194–5
Elgar, Sybil, 221
Employers' Forum, 217
employment, 153, 169–70, 216–7
encephalitis, 63, 69–70, 174
epidemiological studies, 60–1, 80
epilepsy, 28, 58, 69–70, 78, 111, 143–4
exams, 167–8
expeditions, 95
  shopping, 116–7
eye contact, 37, 93

failure, 129, 131
fairy changeling legends, 17
fears, 53–4, 65, 88, 105, 119–22, 134
feeding, 49, 53, 123–5, 136
financial
  benefits, 204–5
  problems, 183
finding and evaluating services, 219–20
food fads, 47, 65, 123
Fragile X syndrome, 68–9, 83
friendships, 166–7
Frith, Uta, 17, 26, 81, 82

games, 139–40
genetic factors, 79, 180, 185

gesture, 24, 43, 70
Gillberg, Christopher, 23, 61, 73
Gould, Judith, 21, 61
Grandin, Temple, 52
grandparents, 184
Gray, Carol, 118
Green Allison, Helen, 221

hair care, 110, 121, 137
hand
  biting, 113
  shaking, 93
Haslam, John, 19
head banging, 45, 113
helping in the home, 137–8
holidays, 57, 96
hospital, 144–5
hyperactivity, 116

imagination, 25, 27, 44–5, 98–9,
  139
imitation, 50
impatience, 18, 88
independence, 54, 59, 65, 162–4,
  168–9
infantile hypercalcaemia, 70
intelligence, 30–1
interest, 33–4, 35
Itard, J.M.G., 17–8, 51

jokes, 42
Jordan, Rita, 208, 215

Kanner, Professor Leo, 11, 19–22,
  25, 29, 38–9, 46, 49, 61, 62, 63,
  64, 66, 79, 81, 83, 92, 155, 221
Kemper, Thomas, 81
Kolvin, Israel, 22

Landau-Kleffner syndrome, 69
Lane, Harlan, 18
language therapists, 195–6, 216
learning 20, 61, 66–7, 80, 82, 87,
  130, 141–2, 161, 208
leaving home, 153–4, 164
leisure activities, 151
letter reversal, 72

lies, 57
lights, response to, 33, 51
Lister Brook, Sarah, 72
living accommodation, 168–9

marriage, 171–2
massage, 196
masturbation, 151–2
mathematics, 55
Maudsley, Henry, 22
McKernon, Tom, 199
medical investigations, 189–90
medication, 110–2, 126, 145, 172,
  192
memory, 55, 72, 81
menstruation, 152
messages, 138
methylphenidate (Ritalin), 116
mongolism, 80
Montessori, Maria, 19
Mortlock, John, 199
motivation, 54
motor co-ordination, 20, 34
movements, 48–50, 67, 71, 122–
  3
music, 33, 47, 55, 93, 140, 146–7
  therapists, 196, 216
mutism, 38, 73–4

National and Local Autistic
  Societies, 20, 125, 169, 170, 180,
  182, 183, 184, 187, 202, 203,
  206, 207, 213, 217, 220, 221–4
National Curriculum, 167, 215
neurological conditions, 69–70
Newson, Elizabeth, 30
noise, 56, 105, 106, 121, 170
normality, 22, 24–5, 55, 57, 65–
  6, 177
numbers
  of autistic children, 60–2, 155
  of boys compared with girls, 63–4

objects, attachment to, 46–7, 65,
  99–101
obsessive-compulsive disorders,
  74, 173–4

occupational
  services, 216–7
  therapists, 196, 216
Oliver, Chris, 115
operant conditioning, 97
oversensitivity, 53, 56, 105, 106
ownership, 113

pain, 52
parents, 22, 34, 63, 64, 78, 94, 104,
  146–8, 154, 163, 178–9, 181–
  6, 190–1, 197–8, 205–6
Park, Clara Claiborne, 127
parties, 95–6
passivity, 33, 36, 94, 137
pathological demand avoidance
  (PDA), 30
perception problems, 73
phenylktonuria, 69
physical
  activities, 49–50, 140–1, 151
  contact, 33, 35, 52, 92–3, 110,
    132
  examination, 144, 189
  exercise, 107, 140–1, 143, 196
  health, 143–5, 188, 202
  punishment, 105
physiotherapy, 196, 216
Pinel, Dr P., 18
play, 25, 35–6, 93, 94, 98–9,
  139–40
  repetitive, 25, 27, 44, 99
  with other children, 25, 44
Powell, Stuart, 208, 215
praise, 160
pre-school units, 206–7
proximal sensations, 52–3
psychiatric
  conditions, 74–6, 172–5
  services, 202–3
psychological
  dysfunctions, 82–3
  stress, 63
'psychosis', 22
puberty, 151–2
punishment, 105, 158–9

Rain Man, 20, 183
reading, 44, 55, 72
relaxation techniques, 196
repetitiveness, 45–8, 56, 67, 99,
  173–4
research, 78, 82–3
residential care
  for adults, 218–9
  staff, 198
resistance to change, 47, 53, 73,
  99–102, 106, 124, 134–5
respite care, 218
response
  to people, 132, 152, 158
  to proximal sensations, 52–3
  to sounds, 50–1
  to visual stimuli, 51–2
restlessness, 56, 115–6
Rett's syndrome, 68
reward, 98, 107, 129
routine, 46, 48, 61, 73, 99–102,
  105, 106, 119, 171
rubella, 69, 71
rules, 158
Rutter, Michael, 22

Sacks, Oliver, 174
schizophrenia, 22, 74–6, 172–3
schools, 150, 153, 157, 159–62,
  207–13
  mainstream, 90, 207–9
  residential, 212–3
  special, 210–2
  unorthodox, 213
screaming, 33, 46, 56, 100, 147
Seguin, Edouard, 18
self absorption, 35, 37, 57
self-care, 54, 135–7, 142
self-destructiveness, 45, 142
self-esteem, 160, 165
Semantic-pragmatic disorder,
  72–3
sensitivity, 170
  to sound, 51
sexual
  development, 151–2, 166–7
  relationships, 166–7

shopping, 56–7
siblings, 79, 94, 178–80
sign language, 43, 70, 71, 98
sisters *see* siblings
sitting, 132–3
skills, 55–6
  basic, 128–45
  special, 55–6
sleep, 56, 126, 147–8
Snoezelen rooms, 142
social
  behaviour, 18, 19, 56–8
  Education Centres, 217
  interaction, 17, 20, 24, 25, 26,
    27, 30, 35–8, 56–8, 92–5,
    157, 159, 166, 183
  services, 204–5
  taboos, 117–8
  workers, 194, 205–6
space, concept of, 90–1
Special Hospitals Authority, 203
speech and language, 117
  bad language, 57
  comprehension, 40–2, 72–3,
    131
  development, 18, 20, 24, 30, 155
  problems, 24, 34, 38–40, 71–2,
    97–8, 172–3, 195–6
  voice control, 42
speech therapists, 195–6, 216
Statement of Educational Needs,
  194, 214–5
Steiner, Rudolf, 212, 219
stimuli, 76–7, 147
sunlight, sensitivity to, 111

Tantam, Digby, 75
tantrums, 46, 65, 108–10, 135,
  140, 142, 150

teachers, 195
teaching methods, 161
teeth, 143, 192
television, 44, 47
'Theory of Mind', 25, 27, 81–2
time, concept of, 88–91
timetables, 89–91
toilet training, 134–5
Tourette's syndrome, 70
toys, 139–40
tranquillizers, 110
travel, 96
triad of impairments, 25, 34–45,
  61, 66, 72, 81, 92–102
tuberose sclerosis, 69, 79, 80

understanding, 105
  experiences, 25, 82, 87, 99
  of disability, 165
  other people, 25, 38, 45, 81–3

verbal ambiguity, 42
Victor, 'Wild Boy of Aveyron',
  17–8, 21, 61
videos, 44, 47, 90, 97
visual
  impairments, 71
  stimuli, 33, 51–2
voice control, 42
voluntary societies, 220–1, 224

walking, 34
'Wild Boy of Aveyron' *see* Victor
Williams syndrome, 70
Wiltshire, Stephen, 55, 56
withdrawal, 127
Witmer, Lightner, 19
word reversal, 39, 73